Angels in My Kitchen

DIVINE DESSERT RECIPES

Caryl Westwood

D1309230

CELESTIALARTS
Berkeley California

ᔡ *This book is dedicated to the angels who have lifted me on their wings of inspiration, as well as to all of you culinary angels, who enjoy a masterful celebration dessert.*

CELESTIAL ARTS
P.O. Box 7123
Berkeley, California 94707

Distributed in Canada by Publishers Group West, in the United Kingdom and Europe by Airlift Books, in New Zealand by Tandem Press, in Singapore and Malaysia by Berkeley Books, and in South Africa by Real Books.

Cover and text design by Brad Greene
Cover and interior illustrations by Akiko Aoyagi Shurtleff
Cover Calligraphy by Jeffrey Brodkin

Library of Congress Cataloging-in-Publication Data

Westwood, Caryl.
    Angels in my kitchen / Caryl Westwood.
      p.   cm.
    ISBN 0-89087-847-1
    1. Desserts. 2. Angels. I. Title.
  TX773.W477 1997
  641.8'6--dc21   97-16036
                                                          CIP

First printing, 1997
Printed in Singapore

1 2 3 4 5 6 - 00 99 98 97

*T*able of Contents

Acknowledgments

*A*bove all, I wish to acknowledge my beloved husband, Sky Wilson, whose open heart and gentle nature have encouraged me beyond words. Your angelic music of the nine choirs of angels has lifted me and will bring great joy for many wonderful years to come.

At Celestial Arts, I wish to thank David Hinds, who believes if a project is fun, then you should do it. David's infectious humor always brings tears of laughter to my eyes. I am grateful to my editor Heather Garnos, whose angelic voice always warms my heart and whose passion for desserts gives me great delight. Heather has been a true jewel to work with. Thanks to Akiko Shurtleff, the highly inspired artist of the cover and angel drawings, for bringing this book to the celestial realms.

I am forever grateful for the heavenly friends in my life who nibbled on sweets while extending light, love, and encouragement. Thanks to Shayla White Eagle and her daughter Leigh Ashley, Joyel and Joseph Burbul, Paul, Colleen, and Everest Bond, Carol Dimeff, Kathryn Atkinson, Doc Harrison, Joanna Fabris, and Lenny Blanc. Special thanks to my mother Joan Herkert, brother Ray, and sister Karen Depeso. To Bob Skutch, who is the bringer of miracles.

Thank you, celestial angels, for your guiding light, wisdom, and joy.

Introduction

I believe in angels. Statues and paintings of angels fill my home and real angels walk with me wherever I am, as they also walk with you. Because I have been blessed with angelic experiences throughout my life, I never doubted that angels exist.

Angels are thoughts of God who bring good cheer, lightheartedness, and hope to our lives. I believe that angels know only love, and that they are here to raise us up by the hand of our own divinity. Angels reach us in moments of despair or when our minds are quiet, so we may hear and receive their celestial guidance. But angels have often been misunderstood. For example, history has sometimes painted a portrait of stern and angry angels who are tall and fierce and apparently ready to shuffle us off to a place I really do not think we want to go.

Before the world began, the light of God filled the infinite heavens. To express his love, God created the angels, thereby expanding the meaning of love for all eternity. In turn, angels, the fruit of God's inspiration, have inspired human souls throughout time and continue to do so to this day. In his wisdom, God sent forth nine magnificent choirs of angels, each exemplifying celestial qualities, and each with its own glorious light to extend. At the beginning of each of the following chapters, I describe one choir of angels and offer a true story of angelic intervention. I believe the choirs are here to gently lift us home to the majestic eternal realm of heaven. If we allow angels into our hearts, they can awaken us from our attachment to the material world and help us tear down the barriers that separate us from God.

As we reach inner peace, we can more easily access the guidance and inspiration that angels have to offer. One day, when my mind was very still, I heard an inner voice telling me to write an angel cookbook. Immediately I began to write, and this book is the result. Throughout the process I felt companionship and the heavenly guidance of the angels who surrounded me. At one point, when the presence felt exceptionally strong, I was moved to look up, where I saw a beautiful aqua blue angel. She was smiling, and compassion filled her eyes. As I raised my arms with joy, she suddenly began pouring out beads of golden light that dropped gently onto my skin. The inner voice spoke once again, saying, "The golden thread woven through all inspiration is to love God with all your heart and soul, as you will learn to love yourself and humanity. Also, be grateful to the angelic brethren who are here assisting in the higher creative expression of this divine love."

Desserts are an expression of love and delight, made to give pleasure. They can help us focus on joy, which is so often lost in our everyday lives. When you step into your kitchen, first still your mind, open your heart, and call on the angels to guide you to higher creative expression. Let's say farewell to guilt and enjoy culinary bliss! God bless you, kitchen angels. Have fun.

TIPS AND RESOURCES

Melting Chocolate

Many of the recipes in this book will require you to melt chocolate. Here are several of my favorite methods:

Double boiler: Before you begin, always chop the chocolate into small chunks. The bowl must be placed tightly over the pot of barely simmering water so that steam doesn't escape and stiffen or "seize" the chocolate. If this occurs, quickly incorporate I teaspoon of oil for every ounce of chocolate. Continuous stirring with a rubber spatula will distribute the heat evenly and prevent the chocolate from scorching. When setting aside the melted chocolate, keep the bowl over the hot water until ready to use.

Oven: When chocolate is being melted with butter or cream, the oven is a safe and easy method to use. The oven temperature should not exceed 250°F (125°C), and the chocolate should be stirred occasionally.

Microwave: A microwave melts the chocolate from the inside out, so the chocolate should be removed and stirred every 45 to 60 seconds. For dark chocolate, set the temperature on high. White chocolate melts faster, so the setting should be placed on medium.

Toasting Nuts

Toasting nuts brings their flavor to the peak of richness. Preheat the oven to 375°F (190°C). Scatter the nuts on a cookie sheet and bake for 5 minutes. To ensure even roasting, toss the nuts and return them to the oven for a few more minutes. The nuts are done when they have darkened a few shades and have a toasty aroma.

Always cool the nuts before chopping, or oil will be expelled and the nuts will have a greasy taste. When processing nuts to a fine consistency, first dust them with a spoonful of flour so you don't end up with nut butter.

Making Clarified Butter

To clarify butter, melt it in a heavy saucepan over low heat without stirring. Allow to stand at room temperature for a few minutes until the solids separate. Remove the foam from the surface by skimming with a spoon or ladle. Pour or spoon the clear butter into a bowl and discard the solids that rest on the bottom of the pan.

Freezing Cookie Dough

If you only want to bake a few cookies at a time, you can freeze the remaining dough in tubes. Take a strip of clear food wrap and spoon the dough in a thin strip down the center. Pull the long ends over the dough and press the dough into a tube with the palms of your hands. Twist the short ends together and wrap the entire roll with another piece of clear food wrap. Place in the freezer until ready to use. Slice the dough into circles, and bake a little longer than directed for unfrozen dough.

Reviving Stale Sweets

To resurrect stale cookies, breads, brownies, and cakes, try freezing the dessert in a sealed plastic bag until firm. Splash a few drops of water over the dessert, then microwave for a minute while watching carefully that it doesn't overcook.

Useful Tools

Because I bake on an almost daily basis, I finally invested in a Kitchen Aid mixer, which is second only to my food processor as my most valuable tool. The Kitchen Aid allows for consistent and even beating of batter, and is less demanding than a hand-held beater. If you use a Kitchen Aid or similar mixer, always scrape the bottom of the bowl every minute or two to make sure all your ingredients are incorporated into the batter.

I prefer Pyrex dishes for baking because they ensure even heat distribution, which makes them superior to metal baking pans.

Purchasing Special Ingredients

CHOCOLATE

The quality of your finished product will depend upon the quality of chocolate you use. Overall, I feel Valrhona makes the finest chocolate. The high quantity of cocoa butter ensures a smooth texture and exquisite flavor. My other top choices are Callebaut and Lindt, which are manufactured in Belgium. The most cost-effective way to purchase chocolate is in 5-kilo or 10-pound quantities.

My first choice for chocolate chips is Guittard's semisweet chips. They are less sweet than other brands, and are very cost effective when purchased in 10-pound quantities.

If your local specialty food store does not carry quality chocolate in bulk, contact the following chocolate distributors:

La Cuisine
323 Cameron Street
Alexandria, Virginia 22314
(800) 521-1176
Among the brands they offer: Valrhona, Carma, Lindt, De Zaan, Coco Barry, and Callebaut. Catalog/mail order.

Paradigm Chocolate Company
5775 S.W. Jean Road
Lake Oswego, Oregon 97035
(800) 234-0250
Among the brands they offer: Merckens, Guittard, Nestle's-Peter, Lindt, and Ghirardelli. Catalog/mail order.

FLAVORED SYRUPS

Originally designed for use in coffee, flavored syrups are the perfect replacement for liqueur in all types of desserts because the flavor extends beautifully. The name brand I recommend is Torani. Some restaurant distributors carry different labels, so taste and see which you prefer. These syrups are also available in coffee houses and specialty food stores.

The First Choir: Seraphim
Burning with Love

The Seraphim are the highest order of the angelic kingdom, who sang in praise around the throne of God as the universe was created. The Seraphs are the essence of unconditional love, and extend the great rays of God to the divinity in our hearts, so we will be reborn in the light of Heaven. Through the Seraphs' transforming fire, our belief in separation is burned away so we become aware of God's eternal love forever expanding through all of creation. Their illumination is crimson for blazing love. They have six wings: two for flying and four to veil their faces in reverence to the Almighty Creator. The ruling angels of this order are Seraphiel, Metatron, Michael, and Uriel.

Chanara spent the day in prayer and meditation. As evening fell and the stars rose in the night sky, a moment of grace swept through her soul. The purity of all-encompassing love filled her heart. The timeless, fearless, all-embracing joy of God echoed through eternal awareness in her mind. A voice that filled all burst forth with, "I am that I am, and you are the center of the universe." The veil of separation had been momentarily lifted, and she experienced the oneness of all creation. She understood that in God, every point of awareness contains the center and the whole. Then the angels appeared—and all she could feel was perfect love. In a moment of clarity she understood that the drama of life was nothing but an illusion. She began to laugh uncontrollably. Now she understands that there is a place within all hearts that is upheld by this grace, just waiting for us to touch and share.

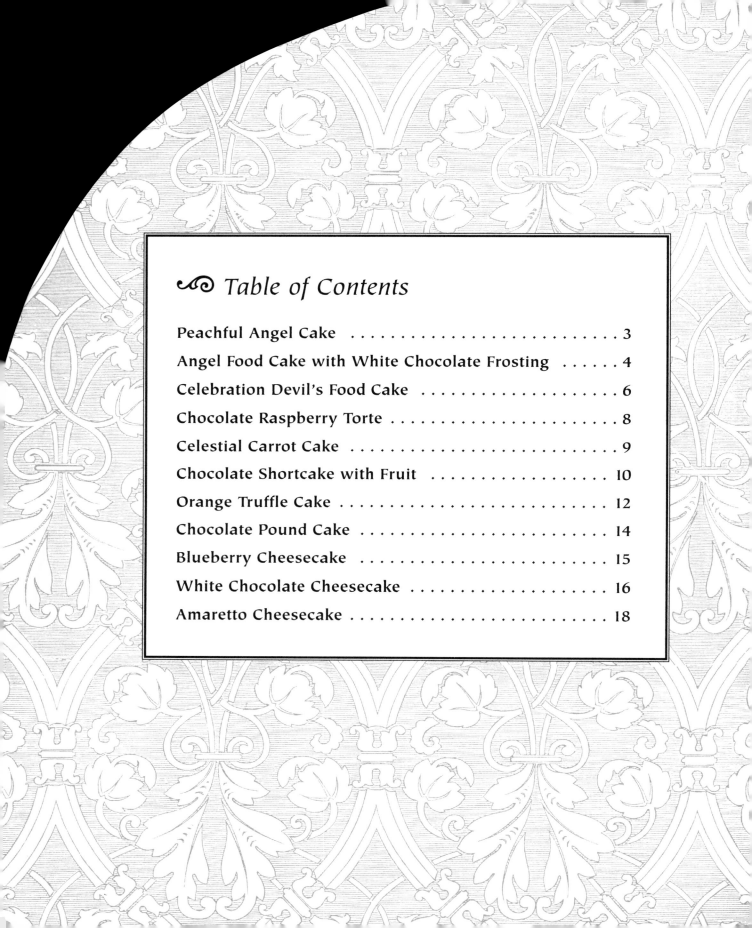

✍ Table of Contents

Chapter 1
Celestial Cakes

PEACHFUL ANGEL CAKE

This is delicious served with a scoop of Mango Ice Cream (page 124) sprinkled with toasted sliced almonds.

6 eggs, separated and at room temperature

1 ½ cups (375 g) sugar

1 tablespoon finely grated orange zest

1 ¾ cups (220 g) sifted all-purpose flour

½ teaspoon salt

⅓ cup (75 ml) peach juice, fresh or from concentrate

Preheat oven to 350°F (180°C). Beat egg whites until foamy, add ½ cup (125 g) of the sugar, and continue beating until stiff peaks form. Set aside. In a separate bowl, beat the egg yolks until very thick and lemon colored. Gradually beat in remaining 1 cup (250 g) sugar and orange zest until light and firm.

In a separate bowl, resift the flour with the salt. With a wire whisk, alternately fold the flour and the peach juice into the yolk mixture, beginning and ending with flour. Carefully fold the egg whites into the batter one third at a time.

Pour into an unoiled 9 ½ x 4-inch angel food or bundt pan and bake for 40 to 50 minutes or until center springs back when touched. Upon removing from the oven, cool the cake upside down by placing the center tube of the pan over a wine bottle weighted down with liquid, or place the cake pan over an inverted funnel. Allow the cake to cool for at least one hour before removing from the pan. If using a nonstick pan, cool on a wire rack. Sprinkle with powdered sugar through a fine sieve.

Serves 12

3

ANGEL FOOD CAKE WITH WHITE CHOCOLATE FROSTING

1 ½ cups (375 g) sugar

1 ¼ cups (155 g) sifted cake flour

1 ½ cups (375 ml) egg whites (from about 13 eggs)

1 teaspoon salt

1 heaping teaspoon cream of tartar

½ teaspoon vanilla extract

½ teaspoon almond extract

WHITE CHOCOLATE FROSTING

12 ounces (340 g) white chocolate

1 ½ cups (340 g) unsalted butter

½ cup (115 g) sour cream

2 tablespoons (25 ml) Triple Sec or orange juice

GARNISH

1 cup (200 g) white chocolate shavings

Preheat oven to 350°F (180°C). Add 1 cup (250 g) of the sugar to the sifted flour and sift twice. In a separate bowl, beat the egg whites with the salt until foamy. Add the cream of tartar and beat to soft peaks. Beat in the remaining sugar 1 tablespoon at a time. Add the vanilla and almond extracts. With a wire whisk, beat the mixture for 2 minutes to incorporate more air.

Gradually sift the flour over the egg whites while folding gently with the wire whisk. Pour mixture into an unoiled 9½ x 4-inch angel food or bundt pan.

Using a criss-cross motion, run a knife through the batter several times to break up any air bubbles. Bake for 40 minutes, or until a skewer comes out clean. Upon removing from the oven, cool the cake upside down by placing the center tube of the pan over a wine bottle weighted down with liquid, or place the cake pan over an inverted funnel. Allow the cake to cool for at least one hour before removing from the pan. If using a nonstick pan, cool on a wire rack.

While the cake cools, make the frosting. Melt the white chocolate and set aside. In a separate bowl, beat the butter with the sour cream until smooth. Gradually add the melted white chocolate and Triple Sec or orange juice, whipping until light and fluffy. Frost the top and sides of the cake, and sprinkle with white chocolate shavings.

Serves 8 to 12

CELEBRATION DEVIL'S FOOD CAKE

1 cup (250 ml) buttermilk, divided

1 cup (170 g) packed light brown sugar

3 eggs, separated (whites in one container, 1 yolk in another,
  and 2 yolks in another)

4 ounces (120 g) unsweetened chocolate

2½ cups (315 g) sifted all-purpose flour

½ teaspoon salt

1 teaspoon baking soda

1 cup (225 g) unsalted butter, softened

1 cup (250 g) sugar

½ cup (125 ml) water

1 teaspoon vanilla extract

CHOCOLATE FUDGE FROSTING

6 tablespoons (90 g) unsalted butter

8 ounces (230 g) unsweetened chocolate

½ cup (125 ml) hot water

¼ teaspoon salt

2 teaspoons vanilla extract

4 cups (600 g) powdered sugar

GARNISH

1 cup (200 g) semisweet chocolate shavings .

Preheat oven to 375°F (190°C). Lightly oil three 9-inch cake pans and dust with flour.

In a heavy saucepan over low heat, whisk ½ cup (125 ml) of the buttermilk, the brown sugar, and 1 egg yolk until smooth. Add the chocolate and whisk until melted. Remove from heat.

Resift the flour with the salt and baking soda. In another bowl, beat the butter with the sugar until light, then beat in the remaining 2 egg yolks until fully incorporated. Beat the flour mixture, water, and remaining ½ cup buttermilk into the butter mixture, alternating quantities of each and ending with the flour. Mix in chocolate until well incorporated, then add the vanilla extract. Whip the egg whites to heavy peaks and fold into the batter. Divide the batter equally among the cake pans. Bake for about 20 minutes or until a skewer inserted into the center comes out clean.

While the cake cools, make the frosting. In a heavy saucepan, melt the butter, then stir in the unsweetened chocolate until melted. Remove from heat and whisk in the water, salt, and vanilla. Beat in the powdered sugar until light and fluffy. If the frosting is dry, add a little milk and continue to whip. Spread the frosting between the layers and generously on the sides and top of the cake. Sprinkle with the chocolate shavings.

Serves 8 to 12

CHOCOLATE RASPBERRY TORTE

*This torte needs to be refrigerated overnight, so be sure
to bake it the day before you plan to serve it.*

1 cup (225 g) unsalted butter

1 pound (454 g) semisweet chocolate

1 cup (250 g) sugar

½ cup (55 g) unsweetened cocoa powder

½ cup (115 g) sour cream

1 teaspoon almond extract

6 eggs, separated and at room temperature

TOPPING

½ cup (165 g) seedless raspberry jam

3 cups (750 ml) fresh raspberries

Preheat oven to 400°F (200°C). Lightly oil a 10-inch round cake pan, line the
bottom with parchment paper, spray oil on the parchment, and dust with
flour. Melt the butter with the chocolate. Combine sugar with cocoa and whisk
into the chocolate. Whisk in the sour cream, the extract, and the yolks.

In a separate bowl, whip the whites to soft peaks and fold into the chocolate
one third at a time. Turn mixture onto the cake pan, set it in a large roasting
pan, and pour in enough hot water to go 1 inch up the sides of the cake pan.
Bake for 10 minutes, then reduce temperature to 325°F (160°C) and bake for
an additional 40 to 50 minutes; the center will appear soft and the sides firm.
Remove from oven and cool on a rack. Refrigerate the cake overnight.

The next day, remove the cake from the pan: place a large plate on top, then
flip the pan over. Peel off the parchment paper. Spread the raspberry jam over
the top, then smother with fresh raspberries. To make clean slices, use a
chef's knife warmed in hot water, then dried with a towel; clean the knife and
repeat the process for each slice.

8

Serves 12

CELESTIAL CARROT CAKE

2 cups (500 g) sugar

1 ½ cups (375 ml) canola oil

4 eggs

1 teaspoon vanilla extract

3 cups (175 g) finely grated carrots

¾ cup (120 g) golden raisins

¾ cup (95 g) chopped toasted walnuts or pecans

2 cups (250 g) all-purpose flour

1 teaspoon salt

2 teaspoons baking soda

2 teaspoons cinnamon

CREAM CHEESE FROSTING

½ cup (125 g) unsalted butter

8 ounces (225 g) cream cheese

3 cups (450 g) sifted powdered sugar

1 teaspoon vanilla extract

¼ teaspoon almond extract or 1 teaspoon maple flavoring

GARNISH

1 cup (95 g) shredded coconut

Lightly oil and dust with flour two 10-inch round cake pans or lightly oil one 13 x 9-inch rectangular cake pan. Preheat oven to 325°F (160°C). Whisk the sugar with the oil until smooth. Whisk in the eggs one at a time, then the vanilla. Stir in the carrots, raisins, and nuts. In a separate bowl, sift the dry ingredients together, then stir into the batter. Pour batter into the prepared pan(s). Bake for 40 to 50 minutes, then cool on a rack.

While cake is cooling, prepare the frosting. Whip the butter with the cream cheese until light. Add the powdered sugar and extracts and continue whipping until light and fluffy. Frost the cake, then sprinkle with grated coconut.

Serves 8 to 12

9

CHOCOLATE SHORTCAKE WITH FRUIT

WHITE CHOCOLATE CHANTILLY

1½ cups (375 ml) heavy cream

2 tablespoons (20 g) powdered sugar

2 ounces (60 g) white chocolate

1 teaspoon vanilla extract

DARK CHOCOLATE SHORTCAKE

1½ cups (190 g) cake flour

¾ cup (190 g) sugar

⅓ cup (40 g) unsweetened cocoa powder

½ teaspoon baking soda

½ teaspoon salt

½ cup (125 g) unsalted butter

¾ cup (175 ml) buttermilk

1 egg

1 teaspoon vanilla extract

½ cup (100 g) semisweet chocolate chips

TOPPING

6 cups (1½ litres) sliced bananas, strawberries, and blueberries

¾ cup (150 g) white chocolate shavings

10

Prepare the chantilly the day before serving. In a heavy saucepan, mix the cream and powdered sugar and bring to a light simmer. Remove from heat and stir in the white chocolate until melted. Do not add the vanilla. Refrigerate overnight in a covered bowl.

For the shortcake, preheat oven to 350°F (180°C). In a large bowl, whisk together the dry ingredients. Slice the butter into almond-size pieces, then cut into the flour mixture until crumbly. Stir in the buttermilk, egg, and vanilla until well incorporated. Fold in the chocolate chips, then turn the batter out into a lightly oiled 9-inch round cake pan. Bake for about 35 to 40 minutes, or until a skewer inserted in the center comes out clean. Cool on a rack, then invert the shortcake over a serving platter.

Immediately before serving, whip the chantilly with the vanilla extract to soft peaks, being careful not to overbeat or the cream will separate. To assemble, mound the fruit over the top of the shortcake. Smother with white chocolate chantilly and sprinkle with the white chocolate shavings. Cut into wedges.

Serves 8

ORANGE TRUFFLE CAKE

2 cups (500 g) sugar

1 ¾ cups (220 g) all-purpose flour

¾ cup (85 g) unsweetened cocoa powder

1 ½ teaspoons baking powder

1 ½ teaspoons baking soda

1 teaspoon salt

2 eggs

1 cup (250 ml) milk

½ cup (125 ml) canola oil

1 tablespoon finely grated orange zest

¼ cup (50 ml) orange juice concentrate

1 cup (250 ml) boiling water

ORANGE TRUFFLE FROSTING

½ cup (125 g) unsalted butter

3 ounces (90 g) cream cheese

3 cups (450 g) powdered sugar

¾ cup (85 g) unsweetened cocoa powder

¼ cup (50 ml) milk

2 tablespoons orange juice concentrate

2 tablespoons (45 g) orange marmalade

Lightly oil two 9-inch round cake pans and dust with flour, or lightly oil one 13 x 9-inch rectangular cake pan. Preheat oven to 350°F (180°C).

Whisk together all of the dry ingredients. In a separate bowl, beat the eggs, milk, oil, orange zest, and orange juice concentrate until smooth. Beat in the dry ingredients until well incorporated, then mix in the boiling water. The batter will be somewhat thin. Pour the batter into the pans and bake until a skewer inserted in the center comes out clean: 30 to 35 minutes for round pans, or 35 to 40 minutes for a rectangular pan.

While the cake cools, make the frosting. Beat the butter with the cream cheese until smooth. In a separate bowl, whisk the powdered sugar and cocoa together. Add to the butter mixture alternately with the milk. Add the orange juice concentrate and marmalade. Continue beating until light and fluffy. If the frosting is dry, add a little more milk.

Serves 8 to 12

CHOCOLATE POUND CAKE

For a dazzling presentation, serve this cake with a slice of Chocolate Pate (page 133) and a drizzle of Espresso Sauce (page 58).

1 cup (225 g) butter

2 cups (500 g) sugar

1 cup (170 g) packed light brown sugar

6 eggs

2½ cups (315 g) all-purpose flour

½ cup (55 g) unsweetened cocoa powder

¼ teaspoon baking soda

½ teaspoon salt

1 cup (250 ml) buttermilk

1 tablespoon vanilla extract

Cocoa powder for dusting

Preheat oven to 325°F (160°C). Beat the butter with the white and brown sugars until smooth. Incorporate the eggs one at a time. In a separate bowl, combine all the dry ingredients. Add the dry ingredients and the buttermilk alternately to the butter mixture, beginning and ending with the flour mixture. Stir in the vanilla extract.

Spread the batter in a lightly oiled 12 x 5 x 3-inch tube pan. Place in the center of a large roasting pan and pour in enough water to go 2 inches up the sides of the tube pan. Bake for about 1½ hours, or until a skewer inserted in the center comes out clean. Cool on a rack. To serve, run a knife along the edges and invert over a plate. Dust with cocoa through a fine sieve.

Serves 12

BLUEBERRY CHEESECAKE

CRUST

2 cups (220 g) chocolate cookie crumbs with cream filling

¼ cup (65 g) melted butter

CREAM CHEESE BATTER

10 ounces (285 g) semisweet chocolate

1½ pounds (680 g) cream cheese, at room temperature

1 cup (250 g) sugar

2 tablespoons (15 g) unsweetened cocoa powder

3 eggs

1 teaspoon vanilla extract

1 cup (225 g) sour cream

TOPPING

21-ounce (605 g) can of blueberry pie filling

Lightly oil a 9 x 3-inch springform pan. Mix the cookie crumbs with the butter and gently press to cover the bottom of the pan. Refrigerate the crust while you make the filling. Preheat oven to 350°F (180°C). Melt the chocolate, then set aside to cool to room temperature. In a separate bowl, whip the cream cheese with the sugar and cocoa until smooth. Beat in the eggs one at a time until fully incorporated, then add the vanilla. Slowly incorporate the cooled chocolate until blended. Gently mix in the sour cream.

Pour the batter over the crust, center the cake on a baking sheet, and bake for 1 hour. Cool to room temperature, then refrigerate overnight. To unmold, run a warm knife around the edges and underneath the crust. Slide the cake onto a serving platter. Spoon topping on and refrigerate 1 hour before slicing.

Serves 12

Variation: Omit the blueberry topping and add ⅓ cup (75 ml) of Kahlua or Amaretto (or flavored syrups) to the batter after mixing in the melted chocolate. When the cake is fully chilled, ladle on chocolate glaze (page 28) to cover.

WHITE CHOCOLATE CHEESECAKE

CRUST

2 cups (220 g) vanilla or lemon wafer crumbs

⅓ cup (85 g) melted butter

CREAM CHEESE BATTER

4 ounces (120 g) white chocolate

1½ pounds (675 g) cream cheese

3 eggs, separated

¼ cup (50 ml) raspberry liqueur or flavored syrup

½ cup (115 g) sour cream

¼ cup (65 g) sugar

TOPPING

1 cup (225 g) sour cream

¼ cup (85 g) seedless raspberry jam

1 teaspoon almond extract

4 cups (1 litre) fresh raspberries

1 cup (200 g) white chocolate shavings

Helpful hints on making a perfect cheesecake:

- Have all ingredients at room temperature to minimize mixing time.

- Cream and sour cream should be mixed in at the end, or air bubbles will expand during the baking process and crack the top of the cake.

16

Lightly oil a 9 x 3-inch springform pan. Mix the cookie crumbs with the butter and gently press to cover the bottom of the pan. Refrigerate. Preheat oven to 325°F (160°C). Melt the white chocolate. Let cool to room temperature. In a separate bowl, beat the cream cheese until smooth and then incorporate the egg yolks, one at a time. Mix in the white chocolate and add the raspberry liqueur or flavored syrup. Gently mix in the sour cream. In another bowl, whip the egg whites until frothy, add the sugar, and whip to firm but not dry peaks. Fold the egg whites into the cream cheese batter.

Pour the batter over the crust, then center the cake on a baking sheet. Loosely fold a tented piece of aluminum foil over the top for the first 45 minutes of baking to prevent the top from browning too rapidly. Bake for 1½ hours, then turn the heat off and allow the cheesecake to sit in the oven for 1 hour more with the oven door cracked open. Cool to room temperature, then refrigerate overnight.
To unmold the cheesecake, run a warm knife around the edges and underneath the crust. Slide the cake onto a serving platter.

To make the topping, whisk together the sour cream, jam, and extract, then frost the top of the cheesecake with the mixture. Smother with fresh raspberries and sprinkle with white chocolate shavings. Refrigerate for 1 hour before slicing.
To slice, warm a chef's knife with hot water and dry with a towel. For an even more tempting presentation, serve on a pool of White Chocolate Sauce Divine (page 60).

Serves 12

AMARETTO CHEESECAKE

CRUMB CRUST

2 cups (220 g) amaretti or lemon cookie crumbs

1/3 cup (85 g) melted butter

CREAM CHEESE BATTER

2 1/2 pounds (1 kg + 125 g) cream cheese

1 3/4 cups (440 g) sugar

3 tablespoons (25 g) all-purpose flour

1 tablespoon finely grated orange zest

5 eggs

2 egg yolks

1/3 cup (75 ml) Amaretto or amaretto-flavored syrup

2 teaspoons almond extract

1/4 cup (50 ml) heavy cream

GARNISH

3 tablespoons (45 g) sour cream

1/2 cup (65 g) sliced toasted almonds

WHITE CHOCOLATE AMARETTO GLAZE

6 ounces (175 g) white chocolate

1/4 cup (50 ml) heavy cream

2 tablespoons (25 ml) Amaretto or amaretto-flavored syrup

WHITE CHOCOLATE ROSETTES

1/2 pound (240 g) white chocolate

1/2 cup (125 ml) heavy cream

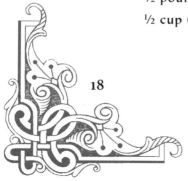

Lightly oil a 9 x 3-inch springform pan. Mix the cookie crumbs with the melted butter, then gently press to cover the bottom of the pan. Refrigerate. Preheat oven to 350°F (180°C). Beat the cream cheese with the sugar, flour, and grated orange zest until smooth. Beat in the eggs and yolks one at a time until fully incorporated. Add the Amaretto or flavored syrup and the almond extract. Gently mix in the cream until well blended.

Pour the batter over the crust, center the cake on a baking sheet, and bake for 1 hour. Cool to room temperature, then refrigerate overnight. To unmold the cheesecake, run a warm knife around the edges and underneath the crust. Slide the cake onto a serving platter. To assemble, spread a thin layer of sour cream to cover only the sides of the cake. Then press on the sliced almonds; they will adhere to the sour cream.

To make the glaze, melt the white chocolate with the cream, then stir in the amaretto or flavored syrup. Let the glaze cool slightly. Ladle it over the chilled cheesecake and return the cake to the refrigerator to allow the glaze to set.

Meanwhile, make the rosettes. Break the white chocolate into small chunks and place in a bowl. Heat the cream until it begins to simmer, then remove from heat and pour over the white chocolate chunks. Stir until the chocolate is melted; return to heat only if necessary. Let cool to room temperature, then chill to piping consistency (about 2 hours). Using a pastry bag, pipe on rosettes and top each one with a sliced almond half-dipped in dark chocolate.

Serves 12

The Second Choir: Cherubim
Splendor of Wisdom

The Cherubim, guardians of the open doors of Heaven, are angels of purity and glory who hold divine wisdom throughout creation. They assist us in transforming our limited concept of self so we can embrace our divinity and angelic innocence. As we reach for the dawn of new understanding, the Cherubim will lift us from our earthly truths to the wisdom of perfect love. They bless creation with a sense of harmony as they sing unceasing praise to God. The holy Cherubim appear in the illumination of golden yellow or sapphire blue, which represent glory, faith, and clarity. The leaders of this order are Cherubiel, Michael, and Metatron.

꧁ Late one evening Erica was driving back home to Mount Shasta, California. She was tired from her long drive and was looking forward to reaching her destination. Suddenly a bright light filled the car. When she turned and looked toward the passenger seat, she saw a beautiful angel looking at her. The angel said "Rejoice, Gabriel has sounded the horn," then disappeared. In her amazement, Erica lost control of the car, swerved over to the shoulder of the road, and stopped. Seconds later a police car stopped behind her and she wondered what to tell him. When he approached, he asked her what had happened. Slightly bewildered, she told the truth. His reply was, "That's weird—you are the third person today with the same story!"

Gabriel is the messenger of truth, resurrection, and ascension. Could it be that Gabriel "sounding the horn" is the coming of peace on Earth?

༄ Table of Contents

Chapter 2
Heavenly Bites and Assorted Delights

CHERUB RASPBERRY CUPS

CHOCOLATE CUPS
½ pound (230 g) semisweet chocolate
30 1-inch (4-cm) pleated paper cups

FILLING
1 recipe Rapture of Raspberry Mousse (page 93)

TOPPING
3 cups (750 ml) fresh raspberries

GLAZE
1 recipe Raspberry Glaze (page 70)

Begin by making the chocolate cups. Stirring constantly, melt the chocolate in a double boiler or a bowl placed over a pot of barely simmering water. Remove from heat, leaving the bowl over the pan of warm water so the chocolate stays melted. Spray oil to generously coat the inside of the paper cups. With a spoon or knife, paint a thin layer of chocolate to cover the insides of the molds, leaving a small paper lip so peeling the paper off will be easy. Refrigerate until the chocolate hardens. Peel off the paper and set the cups aside in a cool place. These can be stored in an airtight container for 2 weeks.

To assemble, pipe or spoon a dollop of mousse inside of each chocolate cup to fill. Arrange raspberries over the top. Brush on the raspberry glaze and return to the refrigerator until ready to serve.

Makes 30 cups

$\mathcal{L}$EMON SQUARES

CRUST

2 cups (250 g) sifted all-purpose flour

½ cup (75 g) powdered sugar

¼ teaspoon salt

1 teaspoon finely grated lemon zest

1 cup (225 g) unsalted butter

LEMON FILLING

6 eggs

3 cups (750 g) sugar

½ cup (125 ml) lemon juice

2 teaspoons finely grated lemon zest

1 teaspoon lemon extract

6 tablespoons (50 g) all-purpose flour

1½ teaspoons baking powder

Powdered sugar for dusting

Preheat oven to 350°F (180°C). To make the crust, mix the flour, sugar, salt, and lemon zest. Process with the butter to a coarse meal, and press into a lightly oiled 13 x 9-inch baking pan. Bake for 10 to 15 minutes or until the edges are lightly browned.

To make the filling, beat the eggs, sugar, juice, zest, and extract until creamy. Sift the flour with the baking powder and stir into the egg mixture until well incorporated. Pour onto the crust and bake for 30 to 40 minutes or until the center is set and the top is slightly crusty. Cool, then dust with powdered sugar. Cut into small squares and arrange on a platter with flowers, if desired.

Makes about 50 squares

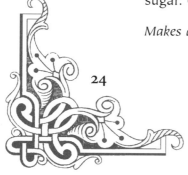

24

SHORTBREAD LEMON CUPS

SHORTBREAD CUPS

¾ cup (175 g) unsalted butter

½ cup (110 g) superfine sugar

2 tablespoons heavy cream

1 tablespoon vanilla extract

2 cups (250 g) all-purpose flour

LEMON CURD

3 tablespoons (25 g) cornstarch

1 cup (250 g) sugar

1 cup (250 ml) lemon juice

Finely grated zest of 4 lemons

4 egg yolks

2 tablespoons (30 g) unsalted butter

Beat the butter with the sugar until light and fluffy. Mix in the cream, vanilla, then the flour until well incorporated. Chill the dough for 30 minutes. Preheat oven to 325°F (160°C). Generously oil several 1¾-inch fluted tins and press a very thin layer of dough to cover the inside of each mold, making a deep well in the center. Bake for about 15 minutes or until edges turn amber and the center is set; the shortbread will puff a little while baking. Cool slightly and remove from the tins by wedging a skewer or toothpick under one side. Always re-oil the tins before adding more dough.

Next, make the lemon curd. In a heavy saucepan over medium heat, whisk the cornstarch, sugar, lemon juice, and zest until thick. In a separate bowl, whisk the egg yolks. In a steady stream, pour the hot lemon juice over the yolk mixture while whisking vigorously. Return to heat and cook until thick while continuing to whisk. Run mixture through a sieve. Add butter, stirring until well blended, and refrigerate until cold. To assemble, spoon a dollop of lemon curd on each pastry and decorate with a candied violet or a sprinkle of powdered sugar.

Makes 54 cups

TOFFEE BARS

CRUST

¼ cup (55 g) unsalted butter

¼ cup (65 g) solid white vegetable shortening

½ cup (85 g) packed light brown sugar

1 cup (125 g) all-purpose flour

TOFFEE FILLING

2 eggs

1 cup (170 g) packed light brown sugar

2 tablespoons (15 g) all-purpose flour

1 teaspoon baking powder

½ teaspoon salt

1 teaspoon vanilla extract

1 cup (95 g) shredded coconut

1 cup (125 g) slivered almonds

Preheat oven to 350°F (180°C). Beat the butter, shortening, and brown sugar until smooth. Mix with the flour to a coarse grain, and press onto the bottom of a lightly oiled 13 x 9-inch cake pan. Bake for 10 minutes or until the edges begin to brown.

In a large bowl, whisk the eggs, brown sugar, flour, baking powder, salt, and vanilla until creamy. Fold in the coconut and slivered almonds, and pour the mixture onto the prebaked crust. Continue baking for 30 to 45 minutes or until the center is set. Cool on a rack, then slice into finger-size portions. For additional flair, drizzle on semisweet chocolate stripes before cutting.

Makes 32 bars

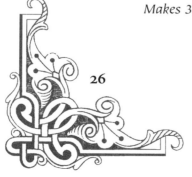

BLACK AND WHITE CHOCOLATE FUDGE

DARK CHOCOLATE LAYER

1 pound (454 g) bittersweet or semisweet chocolate

14 ounces (395 g) sweetened condensed milk

2 tablespoons (30 g) unsalted butter

¼ cup (50 ml) Amaretto or amaretto-flavored syrup

1 cup (125 g) chopped toasted pecans

WHITE CHOCOLATE LAYER

1 pound (454 g) white chocolate

14 ounces (395 g) sweetened condensed milk

2 tablespoons (30 g) unsalted butter

¼ cup (50 ml) Frangelico or hazelnut-flavored syrup

1½ cups (190 g) coarsely chopped toasted and skinned hazelnuts

GARNISH

⅓ cup (40 g) toasted and skinned hazelnuts, finely chopped

Line a 13 x 9-inch cake pan with parchment paper. In a heavy saucepan over low heat, melt the chocolate with the sweetened condensed milk and butter. Remove from heat and stir in the Amaretto or amaretto syrup, then the chopped toasted pecans. Spread evenly over the bottom of the prepared cake pan. Refrigerate while preparing the white chocolate layer.

In a heavy saucepan over low heat, melt the white chocolate with the sweetened condensed milk and butter. Remove from heat and stir in the Frangelico or hazelnut syrup. Fold in the toasted hazelnuts. Carefully spoon the mixture over the bittersweet chocolate layer; smooth flat with a knife. Sprinkle the remaining finely chopped hazelnuts over the top. Return the pan to the refrigerator to set for approximately 3 hours. Cut into small pieces and serve each in a paper truffle cup.

Makes about 50 pieces

$\mathscr{H}$AZELNUT BROWNIES

BROWNIES

5 ounces (150 g) unsweetened chocolate

1 cup (225 g) margarine

2 cups (500 g) sugar

4 eggs

1 cup (125 g) all-purpose flour

1 teaspoon baking soda

1 teaspoon salt

1 teaspoon vanilla extract

HAZELNUT BUTTERCREAM

1 cup (125 g) toasted and skinned hazelnuts

1 tablespoon (10 g) all-purpose flour

$\frac{1}{4}$ cup (50 ml) light corn syrup

1 tablespoon maple extract

4 tablespoons (55 g) unsalted butter

$\frac{2}{3}$ cup (100 g) powdered sugar

CHOCOLATE GLAZE

6 ounces (180 g) semisweet chocolate

$\frac{1}{4}$ cup (50 ml) heavy cream

2 tablespoons (30 g) unsalted butter

2 tablespoons (25 ml) light corn syrup

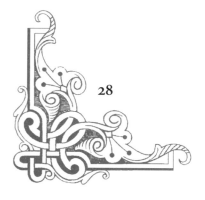

28

Preheat oven to 400°F (200°C). To make the brownies, melt the chocolate with the margarine in a heavy saucepan over low heat, stirring constantly. Remove from heat and whisk in the sugar, then whisk in the eggs one at a time, followed by the vanilla. In a separate bowl, sift together the flour, soda, and salt, then fold into the chocolate mixture. Pour into a lightly oiled 13 x 9-inch cake pan and bake for 30 to 40 minutes or until center is set but still soft. Cool on a rack.

To make the buttercream, process the hazelnuts and flour to a fine grind (the flour will help to keep the nuts from expelling oil). Mix with the corn syrup and maple extract until blended. Set aside for 30 minutes. In a separate bowl, beat the butter with the sugar until light and fluffy. Mix with the hazelnut paste until fully incorporated.

To begin assembly, spread the hazelnut buttercream over the brownies and refrigerate for 30 minutes. Meanwhile, make the glaze by gently melting the chocolate with the heavy cream and butter. Whisk in the corn syrup until fully blended. Remove the brownies from the refrigerator, pour the chocolate glaze over them, covering the hazelnut buttercream, then return pan to the refrigerator for an additional 60 minutes. Sprinkle with crushed hazelnuts or decorate with candied violets. Cut into finger-size pieces.

Makes about 48 brownies

$\mathcal{P}$ECAN CANDY HEAVEN

3 cups (375 g) toasted pecan halves

14 ounces (400 g) good quality white chocolate

2 ounces (60 g) semisweet chocolate

Preheat oven to 350°F (180°C). Scatter the pecans on a baking sheet and roast them in the oven for about 10 to 15 minutes or until medium brown, tossing every few minutes to ensure even roasting. Set aside to cool, then gently shake the nuts in a medium sieve to remove the flakes.

Line baking sheets with parchment paper and set aside. Gently melt the white chocolate, then fold in the cooled nuts with a rubber spatula. Spoon out 3 pecans at a time, placing clusters about 1 inch apart on the parchment paper. Allow to set at room temperature or in the refrigerator.

After candies have set, melt the semisweet chocolate. Dip the tip of a fork into the chocolate, and sweep the fork a few inches above the candies in quick movements to allow streaks of dark chocolate to highlight the white candy pieces. Repeat until all of the candies are decorated. Serve on a platter arranged with fresh flowers, if desired.

Makes about 55 pieces

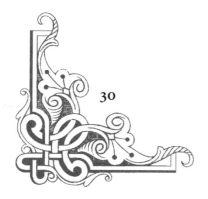

30

TIMELESS TRUFFLES

These basic recipes can be transformed into a vast array of flavors. I have included a few ideas; you may substitute your own flavorings, using similar quantities to those shown in the creative flavorings section on page 34. The chocolate centers can hold a healthy amount of liqueur, which develops the aroma and gives the truffle a bite. The jam intensifies the flavor, and the extract complements the essential flavor. (Be careful not to add excess butter or cream, or the filling will become too soft to work with. If this happens, remelt the filling in a double boiler and add more chocolate.)

It is best to prepare the centers the day before dipping, to allow them to harden enough to be scooped into balls.

When dipping the truffle fillings in coating, if you decide not to roll them in a garnish, then tap off the excess chocolate sufficiently before placing them on the parchment paper—otherwise your truffles will grow "feet." On your first few tries, your truffles will probably grow size twelves, but don't despair—you will catch on. Use a sharp paring knife to trim them up and no one will be the wiser. And don't worry if you can't eat them all: truffles can be frozen for weeks. (My husband actually enjoys them most when they are very cold.)

DARK CHOCOLATE TRUFFLES

DARK CHOCOLATE CENTER

8 tablespoons (125 g) unsalted butter

⅓ cup (75 ml) heavy cream

1 pound (454 g) semisweet or bittersweet chocolate

Flavoring of choice

DARK CHOCOLATE COATING

12 ounces (340 g) semisweet or bittersweet chocolate

1 tablespoon (15 g) solid white vegetable shortening

WHITE CHOCOLATE TRUFFLES

WHITE CHOCOLATE CENTER

1 tablespoon (15 g) unsalted butter

½ cup (125 ml) heavy cream

1 pound (454 g) white chocolate

Flavoring of choice

WHITE CHOCOLATE COATING

12 ounces (340 g) white chocolate

1 tablespoon (15 g) solid white vegetable shortening

To prepare the chocolate centers: Melt the butter, cream, and coarsely chopped chocolate in a bowl over barely simmering water, stirring constantly. Remove from heat and whisk in the flavorings, if desired. Refrigerate in a covered bowl overnight to allow the chocolate to become stiff.

To form the centers: Using a 1-ounce (30-g) scoop, form the chocolate into mounds, lining them up on a baking sheet lined with parchment paper until all of the chocolate is portioned. After the chocolate is portioned, form the centers into round balls by rolling them gently between your palms. Refrigerate or freeze the fillings for several hours to harden. When the centers are chilled and firm, prepare the truffle coating.

To prepare the coating: Melt the chocolate and shortening in a bowl over barely simmering water, stirring constantly. Remove from heat and, if using dark chocolate, leave the bowl over the pan of hot water to keep the chocolate warm while dipping. White chocolate is softer and does not require the additional heat.

Dipping and garnishing the truffles: Set up your work space by placing the truffle centers on the left, dipping chocolate and garnish in the center, and another baking sheet lined with parchment paper on the right. Place a truffle filling on a fork and submerge it into the dipping chocolate, rolling it around until it is fully coated. Lift the truffle up, then tap off the excess chocolate. Bring the truffle to one side of the bowl, sweeping the bottom of the fork over the inside rim to remove excess chocolate, then tap the fork against the bowl one more time. Slide the truffle into the garnish and swirl the bowl in a circle until the chocolate coating is fully covered with the garnish. Allow it to rest for a few seconds until the coating begins to firm up, then place it on the parchment paper to finish setting. Repeat until all of the truffles are coated.

Makes about 32 truffles

Creative Flavoring Suggestions

*D*ARK CHOCOLATE TRUFFLES

BITTERSWEET RASPBERRY TRUFFLES
Use bittersweet chocolate for the centers and coating, following the main recipe. To flavor the centers, whisk in ⅓ cup (110 g) seedless raspberry jam and ⅓ cup (75 ml) Chambord or raspberry syrup. For the garnish, roll the truffles in a bowl of 2 cups (220 g) unsweetened cocoa powder.

ALMOND FRANGELICO TRUFFLES
Use semisweet chocolate for the centers and coating, following the main recipe. To flavor the centers, whisk in 4 ounces (120 g) of crumbled marzipan and ⅓ cup (75 ml) Frangelico or hazelnut syrup. For the garnish, roll the truffles in 3 cups (375 g) toasted, cooled, finely chopped hazelnuts tossed with ½ cup (100 g) grated semisweet chocolate.

PEACH AND AMARETTO TRUFFLES
Use semisweet chocolate for the centers and coating, following the main recipe. To flavor the centers, whisk in ⅓ cup (110 g) pureed peach jam, ⅓ cup (75 ml) Amaretto or amaretto-flavored syrup, and 1 teaspoon almond extract. For the garnish, roll the truffles in 2½ cups (475 g) praline (see page 140).

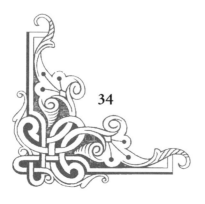

WHITE CHOCOLATE TRUFFLES

GRAND MARNIER TRUFFLE

Use good quality white chocolate for the centers and coating, following the main recipe. To flavor the centers, whisk in ⅓ cup (110 g) puréed orange marmalade, ⅓ cup (75 ml) Grand Marnier, and 1 teaspoon orange extract. For the garnish, roll the truffles in 2 cups (380 g) of praline (see page 140) tossed with 1 cup (200 g) of finely grated white chocolate.

APRICOT AMARETTO TRUFFLE

Use good quality white chocolate for the centers and coating, following the main recipe. To flavor the centers, whisk in ⅓ cup (110 g) puréed apricot jam, ⅓ cup Amaretto or amaretto-flavored syrup, and ½ teaspoon almond extract. For the garnish, roll the truffles in 3 cups (375 g) of toasted, cooled, coarsely chopped slivered almonds.

The Third Choir: Thrones
Divine Immanence

The Thrones illuminate the light of God in our hearts so we may realize Heaven on Earth. They are angels of manifestation who assist us in creating an abundant life filled with joy. Through them we more fully understand that we are an essential part of creation being loved and supported toward our highest achievements. They appear as wheels upon wheels, in the illumination of brilliant gold, which represents the Christ Consciousness of divine will, power, and glory. The ruling angels of this order are Orifiel, Zaphkiel, and Raziel.

I was traveling through a passage of life called "the dark side of the soul." I felt that God had abandoned me, but I did not know why. All there was left to do was to pray for guidance. A slight shift to inner peace touched my heart and then the room was filled with spheres of golden light swaying gently through the unlit room. A sense of Divine Love lifted me from all of the pain that pierced my soul. The angels who appeared to me that night will be my inspiration for life.
—Orphiel

❧ Table of Contents

Chapter 3
Cosmic Cookies

THE KUNDALINI COOKIE

1 cup (225 g) unsalted butter

¾ cup (190 g) sugar

¾ cup (130 g) packed light brown sugar

2 eggs

1 teaspoon vanilla extract

½ teaspoon salt

2¼ cups (280 g) all-purpose flour

12 ounces (340 g) semisweet chocolate chips

11 ounces (311 g) butterscotch chips

2 cups (250 g) pecans, toasted then coarsely chopped

Preheat oven to 350°F (180°C). In a large mixing bowl, whip the butter with the sugars until light and fluffy. Beat in the eggs one at a time, then add the vanilla. In a separate bowl, sift the flour with the salt. Add to the batter, mixing well. Stir in the chips and toasted pecans.

Using a 1-ounce (30-g) scoop, portion batter onto an ungreased baking sheet. Bake for about 10 minutes, or until the edges begin to brown and the centers remain slightly soft.

Makes about 4 dozen cookies

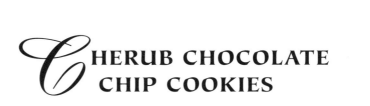

CHERUB CHOCOLATE CHIP COOKIES

1 ¼ cups (280 g) unsalted butter

1 cup (170 g) packed light brown sugar

½ cup (125 g) sugar

2 eggs

⅓ cup (75 ml) light corn syrup

1 tablespoon vanilla extract

¼ cup (30 g) unsweetened cocoa powder

2 ¼ cups (280 g) all-purpose flour

1 cup (90 g) rolled oats, measured and then processed to a powder

1 teaspoon baking soda

½ teaspoon salt

3 cups (600 g) chocolate chips

2 cups (250 g) walnuts, toasted then coarsely chopped

Preheat oven to 350°F (180°C). Whip the butter with the sugars until light and fluffy. Beat in the eggs one at a time, then add the corn syrup, vanilla, and cocoa powder.

In a separate bowl, stir the flour, oats, soda, and salt together. Add to the butter mixture and mix well. Stir in the chocolate chips and walnut pieces.

Using a 1-ounce (30-g) scoop, portion the batter onto a lightly oiled baking pan. Bake for about 10 minutes, or until the edges begin to brown and the centers remain slightly soft.

Makes about 4 dozen cookies

WHITE CHOCOLATE MACADAMIA NUT COOKIES

3/4 cup (175 g) unsalted butter

3/4 cup (130 g) packed light brown sugar

1/2 cup (125 g) sugar

1 egg

1 teaspoon vanilla extract

1 teaspoon maple flavoring

2 cups (250 g) all-purpose flour

1 teaspoon baking soda

1/2 teaspoon salt

12 ounces (340 g) white chocolate pieces

1 cup (125 g) macadamia nuts, crushed

Preheat oven to 375°F (190°C). Whip the butter with the sugars until light and fluffy. Beat in the egg, vanilla, and maple flavoring. In a separate bowl, sift together the flour, baking soda, and salt. Add to the butter mixture and blend well. Stir in the white chocolate chips and macadamia nuts.

Using a 1-ounce (30-g) scoop, portion the dough onto an ungreased baking pan. Bake for about 10 minutes, or until the edges begin to brown and the centers remain slightly soft.

Makes about 4 dozen cookies

DOUBLE BUTTERSCOTCH COOKIES

¾ cup (175 g) unsalted butter

¾ cup (130 g) packed light brown sugar

½ cup (125 g) sugar

2 eggs

½ cup (125 ml) butterscotch-flavored syrup

½ teaspoon salt

2¼ cups (280 g) all-purpose flour

11 ounces (311 g) butterscotch chips

1 cup (125 g) toasted pecan pieces

Preheat oven to 350°F (180°C). Whip the butter with the sugars until light and fluffy.

Incorporate the eggs one at a time, mixing well after each. Slowly mix in the butterscotch syrup. In a separate bowl, sift the flour with the salt, then mix into the batter. Stir in the butterscotch chips and toasted pecan pieces.

Using a 1-ounce (30-g) scoop, portion the dough onto a lightly oiled baking pan. Bake for about 10 minutes, or until the edges begin to brown and the centers remain slightly soft.

Makes about 4 dozen cookies

CHOCOLATE ESPRESSO COOKIES

Serve these with a cup of espresso and a scoop of Coffee Toffee Chip Ice Cream (recipe on page 125).

10 tablespoons (150 g) unsalted butter

6 ounces (170 g) semisweet chocolate

4 ounces (115 g) unsweetened chocolate

4 eggs

1 cup (250 g) sugar

1 tablespoon finely ground espresso beans

2 tablespoons Kahlua or coffee-flavored syrup

1 cup (125 g) all-purpose flour

½ teaspoon baking powder

¼ teaspoon salt

1 cup (200 g) semisweet chocolate chips

1 cup (125 g) chopped toasted pecans

Preheat oven to 350°F (180°C). Melt the butter with the semisweet and unsweetened chocolates, and set aside. Beat the eggs with the sugar until well blended, then incorporate the espresso and Kahlua or coffee-flavored syrup. Slowly beat in the melted chocolate.

Whisk the dry ingredients together, then stir into the chocolate mixture. Gently fold in the chocolate chips and toasted pecans.

Generously oil 2 baking sheets, and portion 1-ounce (30-g) scoops of the batter about 2 inches apart. Bake for 10 minutes or until the cookies are puffed and the tops are crinkled. Cool on baking sheets for 30 seconds, then transfer to a rack to cool.

Makes about 5 dozen cookies

PERFECT OATMEAL COOKIES

1 cup (225 g) unsalted butter

½ cup (85 g) packed dark brown sugar

1 cup (250 g) sugar

1 egg

1 teaspoon vanilla extract

1 ½ cups (190 g) all-purpose flour

1 ½ cups (135 g) rolled oats

1 teaspoon cinnamon

1 teaspoon baking soda

1 cup (160 g) golden raisins

Preheat oven to 350°F (180°C). Whip the butter with the sugars until light and fluffy. Beat in the egg and vanilla. In a separate bowl, whisk the flour with the cinnamon, baking soda, and oats, then beat into the batter. Mix in the raisins.

Using a 1-ounce (30-g) scoop, portion the dough onto a lightly oiled baking pan. Bake for about 12 minutes or until the tops are lightly browned.

Makes about 4 dozen cookies

Molasses Cookies with Orange Filling

1 ½ cups (340 g) unsalted butter

1 ½ cups (375 g) sugar

½ cup (125 ml) molasses

2 eggs

4 cups (500 g) all-purpose flour

4 teaspoons baking soda

1 tablespoon allspice

1 teaspoon cinnamon

ORANGE FILLING

6 ounces (180 g) cream cheese

6 tablespoons (90 g) unsalted butter

1 ½ cups (225 g) powdered sugar

2 tablespoons (30 g) orange marmalade

Powdered sugar for dusting

Preheat oven to 350°F (180°C). To make the cookies, whip the butter with the sugars until light and fluffy. Beat in the molasses, then add the eggs one at a time, stirring well after each addition. In a separate bowl, sift the dry ingredients together, then mix into the batter.

Using a 1-ounce (30-g) scoop, portion the dough onto a lightly oiled baking pan. Bake for about 12 minutes or until crispy. Cool on a rack while you make the filling.

Whip the cream cheese and butter until light. Beat with the powdered sugar and marmalade until fluffy. Spread frosting to cover the bottom of one cookie, then press another cookie onto the frosting. When they are all filled, dust lightly with more powdered sugar.

Makes about 2½ dozen cookies

PEANUT BRICKLE COOKIES

1 ½ cups (360 g) freshly ground peanut butter

1 cup (225 g) unsalted butter

1 cup (250 g) sugar

1 cup (170 g) packed light brown sugar

2 eggs

2 ½ cups (315 g) all-purpose flour

2 teaspoons baking soda

¼ teaspoon baking powder

¼ teaspoon salt

10 ounces (285 g) English toffee bits

Preheat oven to 350°F (180°C). Whip butter with peanut butter until light and fluffy. Beat in the sugars until smooth. Add the eggs one at a time, mixing well after each addition. In a separate bowl, sift together the dry ingredients, then mix into the batter. Stir in the toffee bits.

Using a 1-ounce (30-g) scoop, portion the batter onto an ungreased baking pan. Gently flatten each cookie with the palm of your hand. Bake for 10 minutes for a chewy cookie or 13 minutes for a crunchy one.

Makes about 4 dozen cookies

$\mathcal{L}$IME DROP ZINGERS

1 cup (250 g) solid white vegetable shortening

1 cup (250 g) sugar

2 eggs

½ cup (125 ml) limeade concentrate

1 teaspoon almond extract

3 cups (375 g) all-purpose flour

1 teaspoon baking soda

½ teaspoon salt

1 cup (225 g) green citron, chopped fine

CREAM CHEESE FROSTING

6 ounces (180 g) cream cheese

6 tablespoons (90 g) unsalted butter

1 ½ cups (225 g) powdered sugar

1 tablespoon limeade concentrate

Preheat oven to 375°F (190°C). Whip the shortening with the sugar until smooth. Incorporate the eggs one at a time, mixing well after each addition. Add the limeade concentrate and almond extract. In a separate bowl, sift the dry ingredients together, then mix into the batter. Stir in the citron.

Refrigerate the dough for 30 minutes. Form the chilled dough into 2-inch (5-cm) flattened rounds, then place on a lightly oiled baking sheet. Bake until the edges begin to brown, about 10 to 15 minutes. Cool on a rack. While the cookies are cooling, make the frosting.

Beat the butter and cream cheese until well blended. Whip alternately with powdered sugar and limeade concentrate until light and fluffy. Generously frost the top of each cookie.

Makes about 4 dozen cookies

HAZELNUT TUILLES

These cookies can be shaped into different forms for a variety of uses.

½ cup (125 g) sugar

½ teaspoon vanilla extract

⅓ cup (75 ml) egg whites

1 teaspoon finely grated lemon zest

⅓ cup (40 g) all-purpose flour

¼ cup (65 g) clarified butter (see page *ix*)

½ cup (65 g) finely ground hazelnuts

Preheat oven to 325°F (160°C). Prepare 4 molds for shaping the tuilles. Whisk the sugar, vanilla, egg whites, and lemon zest until foamy. Whisk in the flour, clarified butter, and ground hazelnuts until a smooth paste forms.

Lightly oil one baking sheet for each tray of tuilles being baked and dust with flour. Use 1½ tablespoons (20 g) of batter per cookie, placing no more than 4 on each sheet. Smooth the batter into a flat circle with the back of a spoon or knife. Bake until the edges are browned, about 10 minutes.

Cool for a few seconds while loosening the edges of the tuilles with a thin metal spatula. Working very quickly, remove a cookie with the spatula. Place over a lightly oiled mold; the back of a small bowl or the top of a red wine goblet works well. Working quickly with your fingertips, form the tuille into a cup. If the cookie becomes too hard for molding, return the pan to the oven for a few seconds. Tuilles shaped into cups create an excellent presentation for serving mousse, ice cream, or sliced fresh fruit.

Makes about 10 tuilles

FUDGE NUT BARS

CHOCOLATE GANACHE

12 ounces (340 g) semisweet chocolate chips

2 tablespoons unsalted butter

1 cup (395 g) sweetened condensed milk

½ teaspoon salt

2 teaspoons vanilla extract

1 cup (125 g) toasted walnuts or pecans

SHORTBREAD

2 cups (340 g) packed light brown sugar

1 cup (225 g) margarine

2 eggs

2 teaspoons vanilla extract

2½ cups (315 g) all-purpose flour

3 cups (270 g) rolled oats

1 teaspoon baking soda

1 teaspoon salt

To make the ganache, melt the chocolate chips in a heavy saucepan with the butter, milk, and salt. Remove from heat and fold in the vanilla and nuts. Set aside to cool while you make the shortbread.

Preheat oven to 350°F (180°C). Beat the margarine with the sugar. Add the eggs one at a time, then blend in the vanilla. Mix together all the dry ingredients, then stir into the batter. Spread two thirds of the dough onto a lightly oiled 13 x 9-inch cake pan. Pour the chocolate ganache over this layer, then dot with the remaining shortbread dough. Bake for 25 to 30 minutes. Let cool and cut into squares.

Makes about 40 bars

WALNUT RASPBERRY BARS

SHORTBREAD CRUST

1 cup (250 g) sugar

1 cup (225 g) unsalted butter

2½ cups (315 g) all-purpose flour

WALNUT RASPBERRY TOPPING

⅔ cup (220 g) seedless raspberry jam

4 eggs

1 cup (170 g) packed light brown sugar

1 teaspoon vanilla extract

1 teaspoon almond extract

¼ cup (30 g) all-purpose flour

¼ teaspoon salt

¼ teaspoon baking soda

2 cups (250 g) walnuts

Preheat oven to 350°F (180°C). To make the shortbread, beat the butter with the sugar, then mix in the flour. The dough will appear crumbly. Press onto the bottom of a lightly oiled 13 x 9-inch cake pan. Bake for 20 minutes or until the edges begin to brown.

While the shortbread is baking, make the topping. Whisk together all the ingredients except the walnuts until creamy. Fold in the walnuts and pour over prebaked crust. Bake an additional 20 to 30 minutes longer, or until the center is set. Cool on a rack, then cut into bars.

Makes about 40 bars

APRICOT BARS

Prepare the crumble topping and apricot filling first so the final baking will be faster.

CRUMBLE TOPPING

4 tablespoons (55 g) unsalted butter

⅓ cup (60 g) packed light brown sugar

½ cup (65 g) all-purpose flour

⅓ cup (30 g) coconut

CRUST

½ cup (115 g) unsalted butter

½ cup (125 g) sugar

1¼ cups (155 g) all-purpose flour

APRICOT FILLING

2 cups (320 g) finely chopped apricots

1 cup (250 ml) apricot nectar

¼ cup (65 g) sugar

1 tablespoon lemon juice

Preheat oven to 350°F (180°C). To make the topping, cut the butter into almond-size pieces and then process all ingredients to a crumble.

To make the crust, whip the butter with the sugar until light. Process with the flour to a crumble. Press into a lightly oiled 8 x 8-inch baking dish. Bake for about 20 minutes, or until the edges appear lightly browned. Place on a rack to cool.

Prepare the filling by combining all ingredients in a heavy saucepan. Simmer for 10 minutes over low heat; the liquid should be absorbed. Allow to stand at room temperature for 30 minutes. Smooth over the partially baked crust and smother with the crumble topping. Bake for an additional 30 minutes. Cool on a rack before slicing into bars.

Makes about 36 bars

The Fourth Choir: Dominions
Source of All Lordship

ominions hold divine authority to maintain harmony throughout the angelic kingdom. They are angels who offer wisdom and peace to our hearts through the gentle voice of intuition. The Dominions offer the gift of healing past wounds with the light of forgiveness so we become more perceptive to spiritual guidance. They appear in the illumination of violet, which portrays spiritual purity and perfection, and carry a sword, which symbolizes balance between the active and passive forces of creation. They are lead by the angels Zadkiel and Muriel.

Joyel was fighting depression caused by turmoil in her life. She prayed to God to assist her in forgiving the events that led to her sadness. In a moment of despair, she was surrounded by a brilliant violet light, and peace swept through her heart. Joyel was miraculously lifted to a state of grace where a sense of divine love ignited in her heart, extending through everything in her awareness as a sacred and holy experience. With perfect clarity as a spiritual being made in the likeness of God, Joyel remained in grace for nine days, a time of healing she will always cherish.

☙ Table of Contents

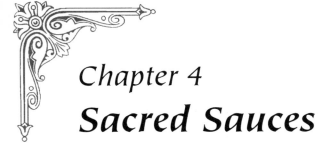

Chapter 4
Sacred Sauces

About Sauces

Just for fun, make two different-colored sauces. Ladle a pool of one sauce on the serving plate, and put the other sauce in a plastic ketchup container with a fine tip. Then decorate the pool of sauce by squeezing flowers, spirals, stripes, or anything your heart desires to make the dessert beautiful. Be outrageous.

Sauces can be made in advance and served slightly chilled or at room temperature with mousses and cakes, or hot over ice cream.

BLACK CHERRY SAUCE

1 pound (454 g) dark pitted sweet cherries

1 ½ cups (375 g) sugar

Juice and zest (cut into wide strips) of 1 orange

1 cinnamon stick

2 tablespoons kirsch

1 teaspoon almond extract

In a heavy saucepan, combine the cherries, sugar, juice, zest, and cinnamon stick. Bring to a boil. Reduce heat and simmer, stirring occasionally, for 30 minutes or until cherry pulp is infused in the sauce. Discard the cinnamon stick, then run the sauce through a sieve, rubbing the cherries against the wire mesh to remove the skins. Stir in the kirsch and almond extract. This sauce is excellent for canning and may be served hot or cold.

Makes 2½ cups (625 ml)

Variation: For Chocolate Cherry Sauce, add 3 ounces (90 g) of semisweet chocolate, stirring until melted. Then whisk in ¼ cup (50 ml) of heavy cream until blended.

55

BURSTING WITH BLUEBERRY SAUCE

¼ cup (55 g) unsalted butter

¼ cup (65 g) sugar

Zest of 1 lemon, cut thick

1 pint (240 g) ripe blueberries

2 tablespoons blueberry liqueur or flavored syrup

In a heavy saucepan, melt the butter with the sugar until light brown. Add the lemon zest and blueberries and simmer until thick, stirring occasionally, for approximately 10 minutes. Run through a sieve, rubbing the blueberries against the wire mesh to remove the skins. Stir in the blueberry liqueur or syrup. This sauce is delicious hot or cold.

Makes 2 cups (500 ml)

DAZZLING RASPBERRY SAUCE

10 ounces (280 g) frozen raspberries in heavy syrup

¼ teaspoon almond extract

1 tablespoon raspberry liqueur

Thaw the raspberries, then purée until liquid. Strain and add the remaining ingredients. Serve slightly chilled or warm.

Makes ¾ cup (175 ml)

Variation: For Chocolate Raspberry Sauce, heat the strained raspberries, then stir in 4 ounces (120 g) of semisweet chocolate until melted. Remove from heat and add 2 tablespoons of heavy cream, then the almond extract and raspberry liqueur.

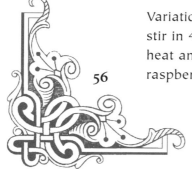

Luscious Lemon Sauce

1 ¼ cups (315 g) sugar

2 tablespoons (30 g) cornstarch

2 egg yolks

1 cup (250 ml) lemon juice

Finely grated zest from 6 lemons

2 tablespoons (30 g) unsalted butter

In a small bowl, whisk the sugar and cornstarch with the egg yolks; the mixture will be very thick. In a heavy saucepan, bring the lemon juice and zest to a simmer. In a steady stream, pour the hot juice over the yolk mixture, whisking vigorously until fully blended. Return to the heat and whisk until thickened, about 5 minutes. Run the sauce through a fine sieve, then stir in the butter. Serve slightly chilled or warm.

Makes 1 ½ cups (375 ml)

Variation: For a smoother, creamier presentation, whip ½ cup (125 ml) of heavy cream to soft peaks, then fold into the cooled lemon sauce.

Butterscotch Sauce

½ cup (125 g) unsalted butter

1 cup (170 g) packed light brown sugar

¼ cup (50 ml) light corn syrup

½ cup (125 ml) heavy cream, at room temperature

1 tablespoon vanilla extract

In a heavy saucepan, melt the butter. Stir in the brown sugar and corn syrup. Bring to a rolling boil for 5 minutes, stirring occasionally. Remove from heat and set aside for 10 minutes. Slowly stir in the heavy cream and vanilla.

Makes 1 ½ cups (375 ml)

GRAND MARNIER SAUCE

2 cups (500 ml) freshly squeezed orange juice

Zest of 1 orange

2 tablespoons lemon juice

⅓ cup (85 g) sugar

1 ounce (25 ml) Grand Marnier

2 tablespoons (30 g) unsalted butter

¼ cup (50 ml) heavy cream

In a heavy saucepan, whisk the orange juice, zest, lemon juice, and sugar. Bring to a boil, then simmer until reduced by half. Add the Grand Marnier, then stir in the butter to thicken. Whisk in the cream, then run through a sieve. Serve warm or at room temperature with tarts, pies, cake, or ice cream.

Makes 1½ cups (375 ml)

ESPRESSO SAUCE

Try this sauce drizzled over Cosmic Espresso Brownies (page 134), mousse, or ice cream.

2 cups (500 ml) heavy cream

¼ cup (40 g) finely ground espresso beans

4 tablespoons (40 g) powdered sugar

⅓ cup (75 ml) Kahlua or coffee-flavored syrup

In a heavy saucepan, simmer the cream with the espresso for 10 minutes. Strain through a fine sieve. Whisk in the powdered sugar until well blended, then add the Kahlua or coffee-flavored syrup.

Makes 2 cups (500 ml)

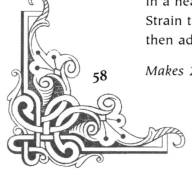

RICH CARAMEL SAUCE

This can be a little messy, but it's well worth the effort. (A word of warning—don't let children near the stove when you're caramelizing sugar.) This sauce is fun to decant in a squeeze bottle with a fine tip. Try it on cakes, pies, and of course ice cream.

2 cups (500 g) sugar

1 cup (250 ml) water

1 teaspoon lemon juice

1 cup (250 ml) heavy cream

Over medium heat, stir the sugar, water, and lemon juice until dissolved. Without stirring, let it boil until it caramelizes to a rich amber color. Heat the cream, then whisk it into the caramel in a thin, steady stream. Serve warm, at room temperature, or refrigerate in a covered jar for up to 3 weeks.

Makes 2½ cups (625 ml)

MOCHA SAUCE

5 ounces (150 g) semisweet chocolate

1 cup (250 ml) heavy cream

2 tablespoons light corn syrup

½ cup (125 ml) Kahlua or coffee-flavored syrup

Chop the chocolate into small pieces. In a heavy saucepan, bring the cream to a light simmer. Stir in the chocolate until melted. Remove from heat and whisk in the corn syrup and Kahlua or coffee-flavored syrup.

Makes 2 cups (500 ml)

$\mathscr{H}$OT FUDGE SAUCE

6 tablespoons (90 g) unsalted butter

6 ounces (170 g) unsweetened chocolate

1 cup (250 ml) milk

1 cup (250 g) sugar

⅓ cup (75 ml) light corn syrup

1 tablespoon vanilla extract

In a heavy saucepan, melt the butter with the chocolate over low heat, stirring constantly. Whisk in the milk, sugar, and corn syrup and simmer for an additional 5 to 8 minutes or until thick and syrupy. Remove from heat and stir in the vanilla.

Makes 2 cups (500 ml)

$\mathscr{W}$HITE CHOCOLATE SAUCE DIVINE

This sauce will add richness to lemon tartlets and other tangy desserts.

12 ounces (340 g) white chocolate

1 cup (250 ml) heavy cream

¼ cup (55 g) sour cream

1 tablespoon vanilla extract

Chop the white chocolate into small pieces. In a heavy saucepan, bring the cream to a light simmer. Stir in the chocolate until melted. Remove from heat, then whisk in the sour cream and vanilla.

Makes 2¼ cups (550 ml)

Variation: When the sauce is finished, add a jigger of your favorite sweet liqueur for additional flavoring.

FRANGELICO SAUCE

Be sure to start this sauce the day before you plan to use it.

2 cups (500 ml) half-and-half

½ cup (65 g) roasted hazelnuts, skinned

6 egg yolks

⅓ cup (85 g) sugar

¼ cup (50 ml) Frangelico or hazelnut-flavored syrup

In an electric blender, process the half-and-half with the hazelnuts for 2 minutes. Refrigerate overnight in a covered bowl.

The next day, strain the half-and-half, discarding the hazelnuts. In a separate bowl, whisk the yolks with the sugar until thick and yellow. In a heavy saucepan, scald the half-and-half and pour it over the egg mixture while whipping vigorously. Pour back into the saucepan and continue whisking until the mixture coats the back of a wooden spoon, about 3 to 5 minutes. Remove from heat and whisk in the Frangelico or hazelnut syrup.

This sauce can be served warm or cool. To serve chilled, transfer the sauce to a cold bowl placed over a larger bowl of ice. Stir until chilled and store in the refrigerator in a covered container.

Makes 2 cups (500 ml)

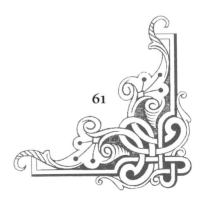

PERFECT PRALINE SAUCE

½ cup (125 g) unsalted butter

1½ cups (255 g) packed light brown sugar

⅔ cup (160 ml) light corn syrup

⅔ cup (160 ml) heavy cream

1½ cups (190 g) toasted pecan pieces

In a heavy saucepan, melt the butter and stir in the brown sugar. Whisk in the corn syrup, then bring to the boiling point. Remove from heat and cool until slightly warm. Stir in the heavy cream and toasted pecans.

Makes 3 cups (750 ml)

ORANGE SOUR CREAM SAUCE

This makes a delicious and unusual topping for fresh fruit.

2 cups (455 g) sour cream

½ cup (75 g) powdered sugar

⅓ cup (110 g) orange marmalade

1 tablespoon orange flower water

Stir the sour cream until smooth. Whisk in the powdered sugar, then add the remaining ingredients. Place in a covered bowl and refrigerate until ready to serve.

Makes 2¼ cups (550 ml)

CINNAMON SAUCE

Cinnamon Sauce is glorious with Deep Dish Apple Pie (page 80).

1 cup (250 ml) apple juice

3 cinnamon sticks

2 cups (340 g) packed light brown sugar

1 tablespoon (10 g) arrowroot

2 tablespoons (30 g) unsalted butter

Splash of Applejack Brandy or apple brandy (optional)

In a heavy frying pan, bring the apple juice and cinnamon sticks to a simmer. In a small bowl, crumble the brown sugar and arrowroot together with your fingertips. Whisk into the hot apple juice and continue to simmer, stirring occasionally, until the sauce begins to thicken. Remove from heat and whisk in the butter until melted. Discard the cinnamon sticks, then stir in the brandy, if desired.

Makes 1⅓ cups (325 ml)

The Fifth Choir: Virtues
Light of Miracles

Virtues are the bearers of miracles that can transform fear to love. They surround us with guidance and protection when our spiritual devotions are anchored on trust and faith in the divine. Angels of ascension, Virtues lift us to the state of grace when our hearts are open to the heavenly powers of love. They appear in the illumination of brilliant blue or aquamarine, which symbolizes spiritual vision and power, and are led by Michael and Uzziel.

"God's Name can not be heard without response, nor said without an echo in the mind that calls you to remember. Say His Name, and you invite the angels to surround the ground on which you stand, and sing to you as they spread out their wings to keep you safe, and shelter you from every worldly thought that would intrude upon your holiness."

Excerpted from "A Course In Miracles," Workbook lesson #183.

Quotation from "A Course in Miracles," copyright © 1975.
Reprinted by permission of the Foundation for Inner Peace, Inc.
P.O. Box 598, Mill Valley, California 94942.

Table of Contents

Chapter 5
Tempting Tarts and Paradise Pies

The following is a selection of some of the many elements that you can use to build tarts and pies. Ask your muses for guidance in mixing and matching to find the flavor combinations best suited to the angels in your life.

PÂTE SUCRÉ

This sweet dough is perfect for pies and tarts.

Single crust for pie or tart, or four 4-inch tartlets

1¼ cups (155 g) all-purpose flour

2 tablespoons (30 g) sugar

½ cup (125 g) unsalted butter

1 egg yolk, lightly beaten

2 to 3 tablespoons ice water

Double crust for pie or tart, or eight 4-inch tartlets

2½ cups (310 g) all-purpose flour

4 tablespoons (65 g) sugar

1 cup (225 g) unsalted butter

2 egg yolks, lightly beaten

4 to 5 tablespoons ice water

Place steel blade in food processor and mix the flour and sugar for 15 seconds. Cut the cold butter into small almond-size pieces and process with the flour in short on-and-off motions until the mixture resembles a coarse meal. Continue with the on-and-off motions while first slowly dripping in the egg yolks, then the chilled water. Processing should not exceed 30 seconds; do not allow dough to form into a ball. Test the dough by pinching firmly between two fingers: if the mixture congeals into a doughlike consistency, turn it out onto a piece of clear food wrap and press into a ball. Fold the wrap around the dough and press firmly into a flat disk.

Refrigerate for 30 to 45 minutes or until fully chilled; the dough should be soft and pliable. If it becomes too firm, allow it to rest at room temperature until it is easy to roll out. Roll the dough out between two sheets of waxed paper. Peel off the top sheet of waxed paper, then turn the dough onto a lightly oiled pie dish or tart pan. Trim off excess dough and shape into desired form. Pierce the dough in several places with a fork.

PREBAKED TART SHELLS

Preheat the oven to 400°F (200°C). Prepare the chilled dough as directed above. Gently mold a piece of aluminum foil to cover; weigh the dough down with dried beans so that the crust will maintain its shape. Bake for 15 minutes or until the edges of the crust begin to appear crisp, then remove from the oven. Reduce the oven temperature to 350°F (180°C). For fully-baked shells, remove the weights and continue baking until the crust is light amber, another 10 to 20 minutes. For half-baked shells, do not return to the oven after removing the weights. Cool on a wire rack.

TASTEFUL TIPS

Cinnamon or finely grated lemon or orange zest may be added for additional flavor. You may also replace the water with fruit juice for extra flavor.

CHOCOLATE CRUST

SINGLE CRUST FOR PIE OR TART

1 cup (125 g) all-purpose flour

¼ cup (30 g) unsweetened cocoa

½ teaspoon salt

⅓ cup (85 g) sugar

½ cup (125 g) unsalted butter

3 tablespoons ice water

Place steel blade in food processor and mix the flour, cocoa, salt, and sugar for 15 seconds. Cut the cold butter into almond-size pieces and process with the flour until the mixture resembles a coarse meal. Continue with the on-and-off motions, slowly dripping in the chilled water. Stop before the dough forms into a ball.

Test the dough by pinching firmly between two fingers: if the mixture congeals into a doughlike consistency, turn it out onto a piece of clear food wrap and press into a ball. Fold the wrap around the dough and press firmly into a flat disk.

Refrigerate for 30 to 40 minutes or until fully chilled; the dough should be soft and pliable. If it becomes too firm, allow it to rest at room temperature until it is easy to roll out. Roll the dough out between two sheets of waxed paper. Peel off the top sheet of waxed paper, then turn the dough onto a lightly oiled pie dish or tart pan. Trim off excess dough and shape into desired form. Pierce the dough with a fork in several places. (This recipe can be doubled for a double crust.)

PREBAKED CRUST

Preheat the oven to 400°F (200°C). Prepare and chill the dough as directed above. Form the dough into the pan, then refrigerate for an additional 15 minutes. Weigh crust down with dried beans and bake for 15 minutes. Remove the weights and bake for an additional 5 to 8 minutes or until center is set. Cool on a wire rack.

$\mathcal{G}$LAZES

With the following process, any jam or jelly can be turned into a glaze. Glazes can be stored in the refrigerator for up to 2 weeks—just heat to a light simmer before using.

APRICOT GLAZE

1 cup (330 g) apricot jam

¼ cup (50 ml) lemon juice or Amaretto

Bring all ingredients to a boil, then run the mixture through a fine sieve.

RASPBERRY GLAZE

1 cup (330 g) raspberry jam

¼ cup (50 ml) orange juice or raspberry liqueur

Several drops of almond extract

Bring all ingredients to a boil, then run the mixture through a fine sieve.

RED CURRANT GLAZE

1 cup (330 g) red currant jelly

3 tablespoons (40 ml) water

Bring all ingredients to a boil, then run the mixture through a fine sieve.

CLEAR GLAZE

¾ cup (175 ml) light corn syrup

2 tablespoons fruit juice or liqueur

Bring all ingredients to a boil, then run the mixture through a fine sieve.

CHOCOLATE FRUIT TARTLETS

DARK OR WHITE GANACHE FILLING

6 ounces (180 g) semisweet chocolate

⅓ cup (75 ml) heavy cream

1 tablespoon (15 g) unsalted butter

or

6 ounces (180 g) white chocolate

⅓ cup (75 ml) heavy cream

1 tablespoon (15 g) unsalted butter

PASTRY

Four 4-inch tartlet shells, prebaked (page 67)

TOPPING

Raspberry Glaze (page 70)

3 cups (750 ml) raspberries

GARNISH

Chocolate Raspberry Sauce (page 56)

To make the ganache, chop the chocolate into small pieces. Melt the chocolate with the cream, then whisk in the butter until a smooth paste forms. Cool the dark chocolate at room temperature, or the white chocolate in the refrigerator, for several hours to a smooth spreadable consistency.

Within a few hours of serving, brush a thin layer of glaze or melted chocolate around the inside of the shells to prevent sogging; allow to set. Divide the ganache equally among the tartlets, then smooth flat with a knife. Arrange the fresh raspberries to completely cover the top of the tartlets, then brush each with a thin layer of raspberry glaze. Refrigerate until ready to serve. Serve on a pool of Chocolate Raspberry Sauce and garnish with sprigs of fresh mint.

Makes four tartlets

LEMON TARTLETS WITH BLUEBERRIES OR KIWI

LEMON CURD FILLING

3 tablespoons (25 g) cornstarch

1 cup (250 g) sugar

1 cup (250 ml) lemon juice

Zest of 4 lemons

4 egg yolks

2 tablespoons (30 g) unsalted butter

PASTRY

Four 4-inch tartlet shells, prebaked (page 67)

TOPPING

Clear Glaze (page 70) made with lemon juice

2 cups (500 ml) blueberries or 6 peeled kiwis

GARNISH

White Chocolate Sauce Divine (page 60)

In a heavy saucepan over medium heat, whisk the cornstarch, sugar, lemon juice, and zest until thick. In a separate bowl, whisk the egg yolks until well blended. In a steady stream, pour the hot lemon juice mixture over the yolks while whisking vigorously. Return to heat and cook until thick while continuing to whisk. Run through a sieve. Add butter, mix thoroughly, and refrigerate until cold.

To assemble, paint a thin layer of glaze inside the tartlet shells; allow to set. Spoon the cooled lemon curd to equally fill all of the tartlets. Smother with blueberries, or slice thin rounds of kiwi and arrange them to overlap, covering the top. Brush on the glaze and refrigerate until ready to serve. Serve on a pool of White Chocolate Sauce Divine.

Makes four tartlets

SACRED STRAWBERRY CREAM TART

For a special presentation, serve slices of this tart on a pool of Orange Sour Cream Sauce (page 62).

CREAM CHEESE FILLING

1 pound (454 g) cream cheese

½ cup (125 g) sugar

½ teaspoon almond extract

1 tablespoon orange liqueur or flavored syrup

2 teaspoons finely grated orange zest

PASTRY

1 10-inch prebaked tart shell (page 67)

TOPPING

1½ to 2 quarts (1½ to 2 litres) fresh strawberries

Red Currant Glaze (page 70)

Whip the cream cheese until light. Incorporate remaining ingredients and mix until smooth. To assemble, paint a thin layer of glaze on the inside of the tart shell; allow to set. Smooth in the cream cheese mixture to fill the shell, and chill for 20 minutes.

Meanwhile, carefully clean the strawberries with a soft brush; do not allow them to become wet. Trim off the hulls. Place the strawberries pointed side up to fully cover the cream cheese. Paint on a thin layer of glaze and refrigerate until ready to serve.

Serves 8 to 12

FRANGIPANI PEAR TART

FRANGIPANI CREAM FILLING

8 ounces (230 g) marzipan

¼ cup (65 g) sugar

¼ cup (50 ml) heavy cream

2 eggs

2 tablespoons Amaretto or 1 teaspoon vanilla extract

PASTRY

1 10-inch half-baked tart shell (page 67)

TOPPING

5 pears, slightly ripe yet firm

Apricot Glaze (page 70)

GARNISH

Several pieces of candied ginger

Preheat oven to 350°F (180°C). Whisk together all of the frangipani ingredients and turn onto the half-baked tart shell. Bake 20 to 30 minutes or until the frangipani is set and the edges of the crust are lightly browned. Cool to room temperature.

To assemble, peel, core, and slice the pears into thin wedges, placing them in a large bowl of water with the juice of 1 lemon. When finished, place them on a paper towel to dry. Arrange the pears in a slightly overlapping spiral over the top of the cooled tart. Brush on the apricot glaze and refrigerate. Before serving, garnish with a few pieces of candied ginger.

Serves 12

74

AUTUMN BERRY PIE

PASTRY

Single Pâte Sucré (page 67)

RHUBARB–BERRY FILLING

4 cups (1 l) sliced rhubarb

½ cup (125 g) sugar

1 tablespoon (10 g) all-purpose flour

¼ cup (50 ml) Grand Marnier

2 tablespoons (40 g) orange marmalade

2 ½ cups (625 ml) sliced strawberries

CRUMBLE TOPPING

⅓ cup (75 g) unsalted butter

⅓ cup (60 g) packed light brown sugar

½ cup (65 g) all-purpose flour

1 teaspoon cinnamon

½ cup (50 g) shredded coconut

⅓ cup (40 g) pecans

Begin by making the pastry. Preheat oven to 350°F (180°C). Line a lightly oiled 9-inch pie dish with the dough, crimping the edges, then pierce the bottom with a fork. Weight down with foil and dried beans and bake for 20 minutes.

For the filling, place the rhubarb in a baking dish, sprinkle with sugar, and bake at 350° for 30 minutes or until tender. In a saucepan, mix flour, Grand Marnier, and orange marmalade into a paste. Drain the liquid from the baked rhubarb into the saucepan and stir over low heat until the mixture thickens. Remove from heat and combine with the rhubarb. Set aside to cool slightly.

For the topping, cut the butter with the brown sugar. Process with the remaining ingredients until crumbly. Place the pie shell on a cookie sheet. Fold the berries with the rhubarb, then turn out onto the crust. Smother with topping and bake for 30 minutes or until the top is browned and juices are bubbling.

Serves 6

CHOCOLATE PECAN TART

PASTRY

Single Chocolate Crust (page 69)

PECAN FILLING

5 eggs

1 cup (250 ml) light corn syrup

1 cup (170 g) packed light brown sugar

5 tablespoons (75 g) unsalted butter, melted

1 tablespoon vanilla extract

½ cup (100 g) semisweet chocolate chips

2 cups (250 g) pecan halves

Lightly oil a 10-inch tart pan, roll out the chocolate dough to cover, and trim off the edges. Pierce the dough in several places with a fork, then set aside to cool in the refrigerator.

Preheat oven to 375°F (190°C). Whisk the eggs, corn syrup, and sugar until foamy. Whisk in the melted butter and vanilla until fully incorporated. Fold in the chocolate chips and pecans. Pour the pecan mixture into the tart shell and place on a cookie sheet. Bake for 10 minutes, then reduce oven temperature to 325°F (160°C) and bake for an additional 20 to 30 minutes or until the center is soft yet slightly firm; the filling will harden as it cools.

Serving suggestions: To decorate the tart with chocolate stripes, melt 2 ounces (60 g) of semisweet chocolate. Dip the tip of a fork into the chocolate and, in fast sweeping motions, run the fork just above the tart from bottom to top. Continue making chocolate stripes around the tart while rotating the pan with your other hand.

Serves 12

CHOCOLATE CHERRY CUSTARD TART

*Garnish with chocolate curls and serve on
a pool of Black Cherry Sauce (page 55).*

PASTRY
Single Pâte Sucré (page 67)

CHOCOLATE GANACHE
⅓ cup (75 ml) heavy cream

8 ounces (230 g) semisweet chocolate

1 tablespoon Kirsch

1 teaspoon almond extract

FILLING
1 pound (454 g) dark pitted sweet cherries, fresh or frozen

CUSTARD
2 eggs

2 egg yolks

½ cup (125 g) sugar

1 cup (250 ml) heavy cream

1 tablespoon Kirsch or Amaretto

Line a lightly oiled 10-inch tart pan with the dough, then pierce with fork. In a heavy saucepan, bring the cream to a simmer, add the chocolate, and stir until melted. Remove from heat. Whisk in Kirsch and almond extract. Smooth the ganache evenly over the dough, then arrange the cherries on top. Refrigerate while making the custard.

Preheat oven to 350°F (180°C). Whisk the eggs and extra yolks with the sugar until lemon yellow. Whisk in the cream and Kirsch or Amaretto until well blended. Place the tart pan in the center of a cookie sheet. Pour the custard over the chocolate and cherries and bake for about 35 to 45 minutes or until center is set. Cool on a rack, then refrigerate until cold.

Serves 12

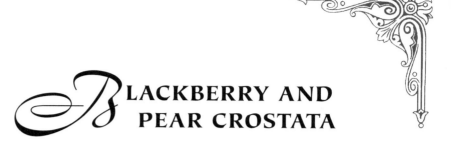

BLACKBERRY AND PEAR CROSTATA

PASTRY

Single Pâte Sucré (page 67), with 2 teaspoons cinnamon added

FILLING

¼ cup (85 g) orange marmalade

2 cups (500 ml) blackberries

3 pears

2 tablespoons (30 g) unsalted butter

¼ cup (45 g) packed light brown sugar

⅓ cup (40 g) sliced almonds

Preheat oven to 400°F (200°C). Roll the pâte sucré into a 13-inch (33 cm) circle. Set on a lightly floured baking sheet or center in a 9-inch pie dish. In a bowl, stir the marmalade to soften, then fold with the blackberries. Mound onto the center of the crust. Peel, core, and slice the pears into narrow strips. Place the pear slices over the blackberries in an overlapping spiral. Fold the dough up over the edges in a pleated pattern. Dot with butter, then sprinkle with brown sugar and sliced almonds. Bake at 400°F (200°C) for 15 minutes, then reduce temperature to 375°F (190°C). Continue baking for 30 minutes or until crust turns golden brown. Cool slightly and cut into wedges. If desired, serve with Cinnamon Sauce (page 63).

Serves 6

APPLE TARTAN

PASTRY

Single Pâte Sucré (page 67)

MARZIPAN CREAM

8 ounces (240 g) marzipan

3 tablespoons heavy cream

1 teaspoon vanilla

APPLE TARTAN FILLING

12 large sweet apples, such as Red Delicious

1/3 cup (75 ml) water

1¼ cups (315 g) sugar

1/2 cup (125 ml) heavy cream, at room temperature

Preheat oven to 400°F (200°C). Prepare half-baked pie shell in a 10-inch deep-dish pie pan. While the crust is baking, prepare the marzipan cream. Break up the marzipan with your fingers. Whisk in the heavy cream and vanilla until smooth. Spread the marzipan cream to cover the bottom of the crust. Reduce oven temperature to 350°F (180°C) and bake for an additional 15 to 20 minutes or until the crust is lightly browned and the marzipan is set.

Peel, core, and slice each apple into 8 spears. Combine the water and sugar in a heavy stockpot large enough to hold all of the apples. Boil the sugar and water until caramelized and amber in color. Add the apples and simmer, stirring, until they are cooked but not soft, about 10 minutes. Remove from heat. With a slotted spoon, lift out the apples and arrange them over the marzipan filling. Pour the cream into the caramel sauce and return to heat. Reduce the sauce, stirring constantly, until it thickens slightly. Drizzle the sauce over the apples. Serve warm or at room temperature. If desired, sprinkle with sliced roasted almonds.

Serves 12

$\mathcal{D}$EEP DISH BLUEBERRY PIE

Follow the procedure in the Deep Dish Apple Pie recipe on the following page, but substitute this blueberry filling.

BLUEBERRY FILLING

¾ cup (190 g) sugar

4½ tablespoons (45 g) cornstarch

8 cups (2 litres) fresh or frozen blueberries

¾ cup (250 g) seedless raspberry jam

1 teaspoon almond extract

Preheat oven to 375°F (190°C). In a large bowl, combine the sugar and cornstarch. Toss with blueberries and set aside for 5 minutes. Gently fold in the raspberry jam and almond extract. Pour into the pie shell and smother with the crumble topping.

Place the pie in the center of a baking sheet and bake for 50 to 60 minutes or until the juices begin to seep through the topping.

Makes 8 large servings

Variation: Instead of a crumble topping, make a double pâte sucré, and finish the top of the pie with extra-wide lattice stripping. Be sure to dot with butter and sprinkle with brown sugar before baking.

DEEP DISH APPLE PIE

This pie is even more satisfying when served warm
with Cinnamon Sauce (page 63).

PASTRY
Single Pâte Sucré (page 67)

FILLING
10 to 14 large sweet apples
Juice of 2 lemons, separated
1 teaspoon finely grated lemon zest
1 teaspoon finely grated orange zest
¼ cup (30 g) all-purpose flour
¼ cup (65 g) white sugar
¼ cup (45 g) packed light brown sugar
1 teaspoon cinnamon
4 tablespoons (55 g) unsalted butter, cut into small pieces

CRUMBLE TOPPING
¾ cup (175 g) unsalted butter
1¼ cups (215 g) packed light brown sugar
1¼ cups (155 g) all-purpose flour
1 teaspoon vanilla extract

Preheat oven to 400°F (200°C). Line deep-dish pie pan with dough, crimp the edges, and pierce the bottom with a fork. Peel, core, and slice apples into spears. As you work, soak the slices in a large bowl of water with the juice of one lemon. Drain the apples, then toss with the remaining lemon juice, lemon zest, and orange zest. In a separate bowl, mix the other filling ingredients together, then toss to coat the apples. Pour into shell and set aside. Cut the butter into almond-size pieces and process with remaining ingredients to a crumble. Press the topping firmly to cover the apples. Place the pie in the center of a baking sheet and bake for 50 to 60 minutes, or until crumble is nicely browned and the juices begin to seep through.

81

Makes 8 large servings

BLACK FOREST DREAM PIE

This delectable pie needs to chill overnight before the topping is added, so be sure to start preparation the day before you plan to serve it.

PASTRY
Single Chocolate Crust (page 69)

CHOCOLATE DREAM FILLING
8 ounces (230 g) semisweet chocolate
1 cup (225 g) unsalted butter
½ cup (125 ml) strong coffee
1 cup (250 g) sugar
4 eggs

TOPPING
24 ounces (675 g) cherry pie filling
1 teaspoon almond extract
1 cup (250 ml) heavy cream
¼ cup (40 g) powdered sugar
12 toasted walnut halves
½ cup (100 g) chocolate shavings

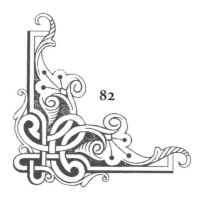

Roll out the chocolate dough to line a lightly oiled deep-dish pie pan and crimp the edges. Prick the bottom with a fork and place the crust in the refrigerator.

Preheat oven to 350°F (180°C). Chop the chocolate into small pieces and slice the butter into chunks. In a heavy saucepan over low heat, melt the butter with the chocolate and coffee. Remove from heat and stir in the sugar until smooth and glossy. Whisk in the eggs one at a time until fully incorporated. Pour the filling into the prepared crust and bake for 35 minutes. Cool on a wire rack, then chill overnight.

Mix the cherry pie filling with the almond extract and spread over the top of the pie. Whip the cream with the powdered sugar to firm peaks and pipe 12 rosettes along the outer rim of the pie, using a pastry bag. Place a walnut half in the center of each rosette. Decorate with chocolate shavings. Serve chilled.

Serves 12

The Sixth Choir: Powers
Balance in Duality

Powers are angels of peace and harmony who protect our souls in the world of duality. As we struggle through our daily lives, the Powers assist us in discovering the spirit of serenity. They are the angels of life and death who ultimately carry us on the heavenly pathway to the Divine Source. They have the power to lift the veil of darkness from our minds so we may know our sacred innocence and the perfection of Creation. Powers carry a white flaming sword that guides us to the light. This order is led by Camael and Chamuel.

Joseph assists people through the death process. On one occasion, Joseph was sitting with a woman who was very near death. Suffering gripped her face, but just before she left her body, a look of joy and peace swept over her tired eyes. She whispered, "The angels surrounding you are so beautiful," then slipped sweetly to the other side.

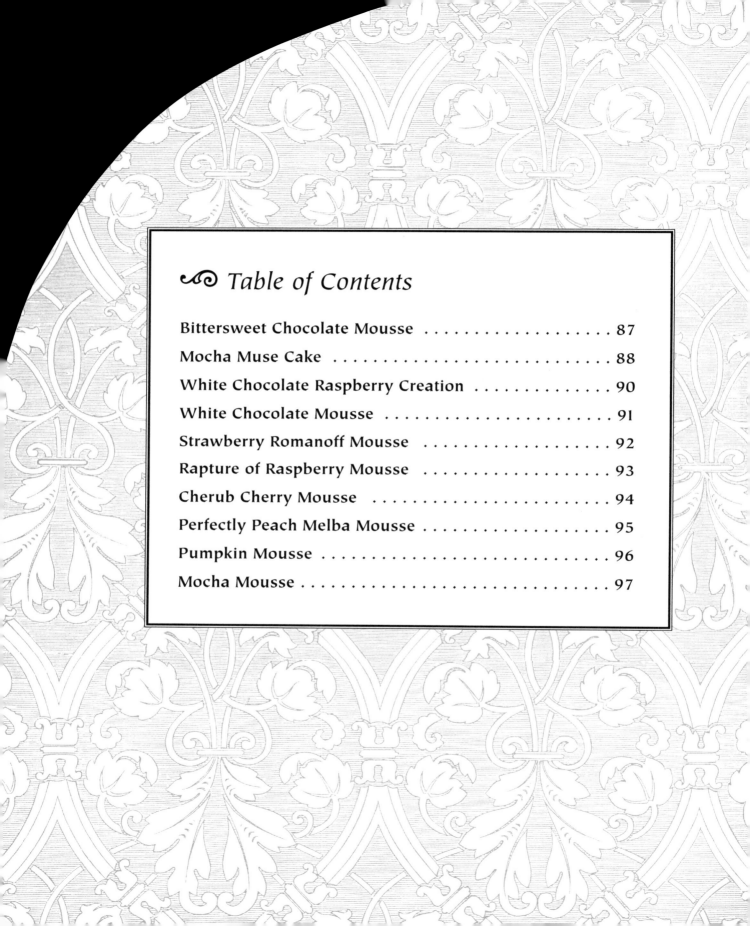 Table of Contents

Chapter 6
Miraculous Mousses

About Mousse

Mousses are very adaptable and can be frozen in molds, chilled in goblets, poured into crusts, and sliced or scooped in a variety of shapes. When scooping a mousse, ladle a pool of sauce onto a dessert plate and, just before serving, when the mousse is set, take a large ice cream scoop or a quenelle mold and place the mousse gently over the sauce. Three or four quenelles arrayed in a star pattern create a beautiful presentation. Mousses are brought to the celestial realms when served with sauces and enhanced with a garnish. Specific sauces and garnishes are recommended in many of the recipes in this chapter. Where recommendations are not given, just let your imagination run wild.

BITTERSWEET CHOCOLATE MOUSSE

Heavenly when crowned with a dollop of sweetened whipped cream and served with a few Chocolate Espresso Cookies (page 43).

1 pound (454 g) bittersweet chocolate

3 tablespoons sweet liqueur (such as Frangelico)

2 egg whites

½ teaspoon cream of tartar

2 egg yolks

3 cups (750 ml) heavy cream

Over low heat, melt the chocolate and whisk in the liqueur. Set aside. Whip the egg whites with the cream of tartar until stiff peaks form. In a separate bowl, stir the egg yolks, then gently whisk into the egg white mixture, being careful not to overwork. Fold the egg mixture into the chocolate one third at a time. Whip the cream to firm peaks, then fold into the chocolate. Divide equally among 8 goblets. Refrigerate for at least 6 hours before serving.

87

Serves 8

$\mathcal{M}$OCHA MUSE CAKE

CRUMB CRUST

2 cups (220 g) chocolate cookie crumbs

⅓ cup (75 g) melted butter

3 ounces (45 g) fresh, soft ladyfingers

CHOCOLATE MOUSSE

1 cup (250 ml) water

1 cup (250 g) sugar

12 ounces (340 g) bittersweet chocolate

6 egg yolks

1 teaspoon vanilla extract

1 tablespoon (10 g) finely ground espresso beans

2 cups (500 ml) heavy cream

TOPPING

1¼ cups (300 ml) heavy cream

¼ cup (40 g) powdered sugar

2 teaspoons (5 g) finely ground espresso beans

GARNISH

1 cup (200 g) chocolate shavings

Lightly oil the bottom of a 9-inch springform pan and line with parchment paper. Toss the crushed cookies with the butter, then press to cover the bottom of the pan. Line the interior walls of the pan with the ladyfingers, the domed side facing the metal rim. Refrigerate while you prepare the mousse.

Boil the water and sugar for 5 minutes to make a simple syrup. Place the steel attachment in a food processor and break the chocolate into small chunks. Pour the hot syrup over the chocolate. (If using a blender, process in two batches.) While pressing down firmly on the lid, begin processing until the chocolate becomes a smooth paste. Add the yolks one at a time, then the vanilla and espresso. Set aside to cool to room temperature. In a separate bowl, whip the cream until stiff peaks form, and fold into the chocolate one third at a time. Pour into the prepared springform pan and freeze until hard, usually overnight. Remove the cake from the pan and peel off the parchment paper. Place on a serving platter.

Whip the cream with an electric mixer, slowly adding the powdered sugar and espresso, then beating on medium speed until heavy peaks form.

To assemble, spread a thin layer of the whipped cream over the top of the cake. With a pastry bag, pipe on rosettes of the remaining cream and garnish with chocolate shavings. Refrigerate for 1 hour before serving to soften the mousse.

Serves 12

Variation: For strawberry mousse cake, omit the espresso. Clean and hull 1 pint (500 ml) of strawberries and place pointed side up on the bottom of the crust before pouring in the chocolate mousse. Garnish with the whipped cream and chocolate shavings.

ABOUT MUSES
Muses are light beings who dwell in the realm of imagination and intellect. They offer inspiration to people who use creative energy. When you are in the mood to develop new ideas, call on the muses for guidance.

WHITE CHOCOLATE RASPBERRY CREATION

CRUST

2 cups (220 g) lemon cookie crumbs

⅓ cup (75 g) unsalted butter, melted

WHITE CHOCOLATE MOUSSE

12 ounces (340 g) white chocolate

10 egg whites

¼ cup (65 g) sugar

3 tablespoons Cointreau or orange-flavored syrup

1¾ cups (425 ml) heavy cream

1 cup (250 ml) fresh raspberries

GARNISH

White chocolate curls

Additional raspberries

Dazzling Raspberry Sauce (page 56)

Lightly oil the bottom of a 9-inch springform pan and line with parchment paper. Mix the cookie crumbs with the butter and gently press to cover the bottom of the pan. Refrigerate while you prepare the mousse.

Melt the white chocolate and set aside to cool. Whip the egg whites until foamy, then add the sugar and whip until soft peaks form. Fold in the chocolate and liqueur or syrup. In a separate bowl, whip the cream to soft peaks and fold into the white chocolate mixture one third at a time. Gently fold in the raspberries, being careful not to break them up. Pour the mousse onto the prepared crust, then smooth flat with a spatula. Freeze 8 or more hours, until firm. Remove from the pan and peel off the parchment paper. Serve each slice on a pool of Raspberry Sauce. Decorate with white chocolate curls and fresh raspberries.

90   *Serves 12*

$\mathcal{W}$HITE CHOCOLATE MOUSSE

White chocolate is very versatile and adapts well to a variety of flavored liqueurs. This mousse is delicious served frozen, and should then be made the day before serving to give it time to freeze.

1 pound (454 g) white chocolate
¼ cup (50 ml) water
3 tablespoons sweet liqueur
3 cups (750 ml) heavy cream

In a bowl placed over simmering water, melt the white chocolate with the water. Remove from heat and whisk in your liqueur of choice. Cool to room temperature. Whip the cream to stiff peaks and fold into the white chocolate one third at a time. Refrigerate for at least 3 hours before serving.

Serving suggestions: Pour the mousse into goblets and chill, or mold into mounds with an ice cream scoop and serve on a pool of sauce. Accentuate with white and dark chocolate shavings and pieces of fresh fruit.

Flavoring recommendations:
- Add your favorite sweet liqueur and serve the mousse on White Chocolate Sauce Divine (page 60).
- Flavor with Frangelico and serve with Frangelico Sauce (page 61).
- Flavor with Cointreau and serve with Grand Marnier Sauce (page 58).
- Flavor with Kahlua and serve with Espresso Sauce (page 58).
- Flavor with Chambord and serve with Dazzling Raspberry Sauce (page 56).
- Flavor with Cherry Suisse and serve with Black Cherry Sauce (page 55).

Serves 8 to 10

STRAWBERRY
ROMANOFF MOUSSE

This mousse is especially lovely when served on a pool of
Grand Marnier Sauce (page 58). Garnish with sliced strawberries
arranged in a fan shape.

3 cups (750 ml) strawberries, washed and hulled

½ cup (75 g) powdered sugar

1 tablespoon (10 g) unflavored gelatin

¼ cup (50 ml) orange juice

¼ cup (50 ml) Cointreau

2 cups (500 ml) heavy cream

Purée the strawberries and sugar. In a heavy saucepan, soften the gelatin
with the orange juice. Place the pan over low heat and cook until the gelatin
melts. Add the strawberries and stir for 1 minute. Remove from heat. Whisk in
the Cointreau. Chill until the mixture begins to thicken. In a separate bowl,
whip the cream to stiff peaks. Gently fold in the strawberries one third at a
time. Freeze in a covered bowl until set.

Serves 6

RAPTURE OF RASPBERRY MOUSSE

Try serving scoops of chilled mousse on pools of Chocolate Raspberry Sauce (page 56). Garnish with a sprinkle of fresh raspberries.

2 cups (500 ml) raspberries

¾ cup (190 g) sugar

1 tablespoon (10 g) unflavored gelatin

¼ cup (50 ml) orange juice

2 egg yolks

2 tablespoons raspberry liqueur

½ teaspoon almond extract

2 cups (500 ml) heavy cream

Purée the raspberries with the sugar and rub through a fine sieve to remove the seeds. In a heavy saucepan, soften the gelatin with the orange juice. Place the pan over low heat and cook until the gelatin melts. Add the raspberries and stir for one minute. Remove from heat.

In a separate bowl, whisk the egg yolks until blended; pour the hot raspberry mixture over the yolks in a thin stream while whisking vigorously. Return to heat and whisk for 1 minute. Remove from heat and stir for 2 minutes to cool slightly. Add the raspberry liqueur and almond extract and chill until the mixture begins to thicken. Whip the cream to stiff peaks, then fold in the raspberry mixture one third at a time. Chill until set, about 6 hours.

Serves 6

$\mathcal{C}$HERUB CHERRY MOUSSE

Slices or scoops of this mousse are truly out of this world when served on White Chocolate Sauce Divine (page 60). As a garnish, use fresh cherries with stems.

1 pound (454 g) fresh or frozen pitted bing cherries

1 cup (250 g) sugar

1 tablespoon (10 g) unflavored gelatin

½ cup (125 ml) orange juice

1 teaspoon almond extract

1 tablespoon Kirsch

3 egg whites

¼ cup (65 grams) sugar

2 cups (500 ml) heavy cream

In a heavy saucepan, mash the cherries with the sugar and macerate for 5 minutes. Over medium heat, simmer until the cherries become syrupy, about 20 minutes. Run through a sieve to remove the skins. Soften the gelatin with the orange juice, then add to the cherry pulp. Return to heat and whisk until the gelatin is melted.

Stir in the almond extract and Kirsch and refrigerate until cold.

In a separate bowl, whip the egg whites until frothy. Continue whipping, while slowly adding the sugar, to firm peaks. Fold into chilled cherry sauce. Whip the cream until stiff peaks form and fold into the cherry mixture one third at a time. Pour into a lightly oiled 2-quart mold and freeze overnight.

Serves 8

PERFECTLY PEACH MELBA MOUSSE

1 tablespoon (10 g) unflavored gelatin

⅓ cup (75 ml) orange juice

¾ cup (190 g) sugar

1 tablespoon lemon juice

2 egg yolks

2 cups (500 ml) peach purée (about 2 large or 3 medium ripe peaches)

¼ teaspoon almond extract

2 tablespoons Amaretto

2 cups (500 ml) heavy cream

Dazzling Raspberry Sauce (page 56)

In a heavy saucepan, soften the gelatin with the orange juice. Place the pan over low heat until the gelatin melts, then add the sugar and lemon juice and stir for 1 minute. Remove from heat.

In a separate bowl, lightly whisk the egg yolks until blended. Pour the hot gelatin mixture over the yolks in a steady stream while whisking vigorously, then return to heat and stir for 1 to 2 more minutes. Stir in the peach purée, almond extract, and Amaretto. Set aside to cool.

Whip the cream until stiff peaks form and fold into the peach mixture one third at time. Refrigerate at least 6 hours before using or freeze until firm. Serve scooped on a pool of Raspberry Sauce. Garnish with a few spears of fresh sliced peach and several raspberries, if desired.

Serves 6

Variation: Make tartlets filled with semisweet chocolate ganache (page 71). Add a scoop of peach mousse over the top, and serve on a pool of Dazzling Raspberry Sauce. Garnish with fresh raspberries.

PUMPKIN MOUSSE

This is wonderful on Thanksgiving Day instead of the usual pumpkin pie. Serve scoops of mousse on a pool of Frangelico Sauce (pg 61) garnished with candied walnuts.

½ cup (125 ml) pure maple syrup

2 egg yolks

15 ounces (425 g) pumpkin purée

⅓ cup (75 ml) Frangelico or hazelnut syrup

1 teaspoon cinnamon

1 teaspoon nutmeg

1 teaspoon allspice

½ teaspoon mace

2 teaspoons vanilla extract

1½ cups (375 ml) heavy cream

In a heavy saucepan over low heat, whisk the maple syrup with the egg yolks and bring to a simmer while stirring constantly. Set aside to cool. Whisk the pumpkin purée with the maple syrup mixture and all the remaining ingredients except the cream. Whip the cream to firm peaks and fold into the pumpkin mixture one third at a time. Chill for at least 4 hours to allow the flavors to blend.

Serves 6

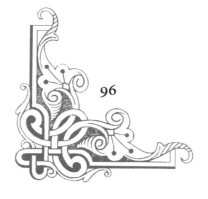

96

MOCHA MOUSSE

For the ultimate coffee-lover's experience, serve scoops of mousse on pools of Espresso Sauce (page 58), garnished with chocolate-covered espresso beans and chocolate curls.

½ cup (125 g) sugar

½ cup (125 ml) strong coffee

8 ounces (230 g) semisweet chocolate

¼ cup (50 ml) Kahlua or coffee-flavored syrup

2 egg yolks

4 egg whites

1 cup (250 ml) heavy cream

1 tablespoon vanilla extract

In a heavy saucepan over low heat, dissolve the sugar with coffee. Chop the chocolate into small pieces and add to the pan. Stir until the chocolate melts. Remove from heat and whisk in the Kahlua or coffee-flavored syrup. Add the egg yolks, whisking until blended. Cool to room temperature.

In a separate bowl, beat the egg whites to soft peaks. Fold into the chocolate. Whip the cream to stiff peaks, adding the vanilla toward the end, then fold into the chocolate one third at a time. Chill for 6 hours before serving.

Serves 6

The Seventh Choir: Principalities
Fulfillment of the Divine Plan

The angels of Principalities are guardians of mass consciousness who gently guide all groups to become aware of the Divine Plan of Unity, which embraces the universe with the wholeness of God. The Principalities offer insight into our personality struggles, where in time we will discover that separation is only an idea that prevents us from knowing God's perfect love, which is all-encompassing. The Princes appear to us in human form. Hebrews 13:2 warns, "Be not forgetful to entertain strangers: for thereby some have entertained angels unawares." The leaders of this realm are Anael and Remiel.

As she prepared to take an insurance exam she needed to pass in order to support her family, Harriette prayed for a miracle for the first time in her life. Just outside the building where the examination was to be held, she saw a homeless man who appeared to have been living on the streets for some time. He looked directly into her eyes and said, "Do not worry about passing your exam. You have always been able to access the higher plains of consciousness!" After the test, Harriette returned to the angel to express her gratitude. The angel peered into her eyes and held up his palm, signaling that the miracle was given and Harriette should go in peace.

❧ Table of Contents

Chapter 7
Metaphysical Muffins and Blessed Breads

About Bread

All the recipes in this chapter call for large eggs and unsalted butter. To ensure that your bread turns out light and soft, with a fine texture, beat the butter and sugar on slow speed for 10 to 15 minutes. For a slight variation in flavor, whole-wheat pastry flour can be substituted for all-purpose flour in equal proportions.

In all cases, preheat the oven and fold the dry ingredients in last. The leavening will begin to react as soon as it is moistened, and the bread may not rise perfectly if the baking soda or powder has already reacted before going into the oven. For muffins, spray a light mist of oil in paper cups or tins, then use an ice cream scoop to portion the batter.

ZUCCHINI BREAD

3 eggs

1 cup (250 ml) canola oil

1 tablespoon vanilla extract

1¼ cups (315 g) sugar

3 cups (375 g) all-purpose flour

1 teaspoon baking soda

¼ teaspoon baking powder

2 teaspoons salt

1 tablespoon cinnamon

1 teaspoon nutmeg

3 cups (750 ml) grated zucchini

Preheat oven to 350°F (180°C). Whisk the eggs with the oil and vanilla, then add the sugar. In a separate bowl, sift all the dry ingredients together, then fold into the batter. Stir in the zucchini until well blended. Pour the batter into a lightly oiled loaf pan. Center the pan on a baking sheet and bake for about 1 hour, or until the top is golden brown and a skewer comes out clean. Before slicing, cool on a wire rack until just slightly warm.

Makes one 9-inch loaf

PERFECT PUMPKIN CARROT BREAD

This bread will remain moist for days.

1 cup (285 g) pumpkin purée

⅓ cup (75 ml) canola oil

2 eggs

1 teaspoon vanilla extract

1¼ cups (315 g) sugar

¼ cup (50 ml) orange juice

1½ cups (375 ml) grated carrots

1¾ cups (220 g) all-purpose flour

2 teaspoons baking soda

½ teaspoon salt

¾ teaspoon cinnamon

¼ teaspoon nutmeg

¼ teaspoon mace

Preheat oven to 350°F (180°C). Whisk the pumpkin with the oil, eggs, vanilla, sugar, and orange juice. Stir in the carrots. In a separate bowl, sift all the dry ingredients together and fold into the batter. Pour the batter into a lightly oiled loaf pan. Center the pan on a baking sheet and bake for about 1 hour or until a skewer comes out clean. Cool on a rack before slicing.

Makes one 9-inch loaf

BANANA POPPY SEED BREAD

This bread also makes a very good french toast to top with maple syrup.

¼ cup (50 ml) canola oil

¾ cup (190 g) sugar

¼ cup (45 g) packed light brown sugar

3 medium ripe bananas, mashed

1 egg

1 teaspoon maple or vanilla extract

⅓ cup (75 g) whole-milk yogurt

¼ cup (50 ml) poppy seeds

2 cups (250 g) all-purpose flour

1½ teaspoons baking powder

1½ teaspoons baking soda

½ teaspoon salt

Preheat oven to 350°F (180°C). Whisk the oil with the white and brown sugars, then add the mashed bananas. Beat in the egg, extract, and yogurt, then the poppy seeds. In a separate bowl, sift all the dry ingredients together, then fold into the batter. Pour the batter into a lightly oiled loaf pan. Center the pan on a baking sheet and bake for 1 hour or until the top is golden brown and a skewer comes out clean. Cool on a wire rack for 20 minutes before serving.

Makes one 9-inch loaf

ORANGE BLOSSOM BLACKBERRY BREAD

This tea bread makes excellent french toast to serve with Orange Sour Cream Sauce (page 62).

CRUMBLE TOPPING

1 cup (125 g) walnuts or pecans

½ cup (65 g) all-purpose flour

⅓ cup (60 g) packed light brown sugar

½ cup (125 g) unsalted butter

BREAD

1-pound (454-g) can blackberries in heavy syrup

1½ cups (375 g) sugar

Finely grated zest and juice from 1 orange

1 teaspoon almond extract

½ cup (125 ml) canola oil

3 eggs

1 cup (250 ml) buttermilk

4 cups (500 g) all-purpose flour

1 tablespoon baking powder

½ teaspoon baking soda

1 teaspoon salt

ORANGE GLAZE

1½ cups (225 g) powdered sugar

⅓ cup (75 ml) orange juice

Preheat oven to 350°F (180°C). To make the crumble topping, process the nuts and flour with the brown sugar. Cut the butter into almond-size pieces and process with flour mixture to a coarse grain. Set aside.

Process the blackberries with the syrup in a blender, then run through a sieve to remove the seeds. In a large bowl, whisk the blackberries with the sugar, juice, zest, almond extract, oil, eggs, and buttermilk until smooth and creamy. In a separate bowl, sift together the flour, baking powder, soda, and salt. Mix into the blackberry batter. Turn out onto 2 lightly oiled 9-inch loaf pans. Sprinkle the crumble topping equally to cover. Center the pans on a baking sheet and bake for about 1 hour, or until a skewer comes out clean. Set on a rack while you prepare the orange glaze.

Whisk together the powdered sugar and orange juice. Pierce the bread in several places with a skewer, then spoon on the glaze until it is all absorbed. Cool for 20 minutes before slicing.

Makes two 9-inch loaves

DAZZLING RASPBERRY BREAD

BREAD

10 ounces (285 g) frozen raspberries in heavy syrup, thawed

½ cup (125 ml) canola oil

1 cup (250 g) sugar

2 tablespoons (40 g) orange marmalade

1 teaspoon almond extract

2 eggs

⅓ cup (75 ml) buttermilk

2¼ cups (280 g) all-purpose flour

1 teaspoon cinnamon

¼ teaspoon salt

½ teaspoon baking powder

GLAZE

Reserved raspberry syrup

¼ cup (40 g) powdered sugar

Preheat oven to 350°F (180°C). Strain the raspberries, reserving the syrup. Set the berries aside. Whisk the oil with the sugar, marmalade, almond extract, and eggs, then add the buttermilk. In a separate bowl, sift the dry ingredients together, then stir into the batter. Fold in the raspberries. Pour the batter into a lightly oiled 9-inch loaf pan, and center the pan on a baking sheet. Bake for about 1 hour or until a skewer comes out clean. Cool on a rack.

Whisk together the raspberry syrup and powdered sugar until smooth. While the bread is still warm, pierce in several places with a skewer and ladle the glaze over the top until absorbed.

Makes one 9-inch loaf

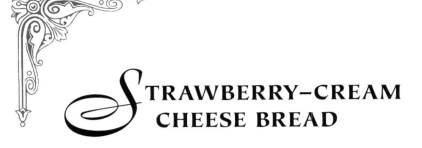

STRAWBERRY–CREAM CHEESE BREAD

STRAWBERRY BATTER

½ cup (125 g) unsalted butter

1 cup (250 g) sugar

2 eggs

2¼ cups (280 g) all-purpose flour

1 teaspoon baking powder

1 teaspoon baking soda

½ teaspoon salt

10 ounces (285 g) frozen strawberries in heavy syrup,
     thawed; reserve ¼ cup (50 ml) syrup for cream cheese filling

CREAM CHEESE FILLING

8 ounces (230 g) cream cheese

¼ cup (50 ml) reserved strawberry syrup

1 egg

2 tablespoons (15 g) all-purpose flour

Preheat oven to 350°F (180°C). Beat the butter with the sugar. Incorporate the eggs one at a time. Sift the dry ingredients together and mix into the batter alternately with the strawberries and syrup. In a separate bowl, make the cream cheese filling. Beat the cream cheese with the reserved strawberry syrup until smooth. Beat in the egg, then stir in the flour until fully incorporated.

Spread half the batter on the bottom of a lightly oiled 9-inch loaf pan. Pour on the cream cheese mixture to cover. Carefully spoon the remaining batter over the cream cheese; it will smooth out during baking. Center the pan on a cookie sheet and bake for about 1 hour and 10 minutes, or until the top is golden and bounces back when lightly touched. Cool on a rack for 15 minutes, remove from the pan, then cool to room temperature before slicing.

Makes one 9-inch loaf

*L*EMON GINGERBREAD

GINGERBREAD

¼ cup (55 g) unsalted butter

4 ounces (120 g) chopped candied ginger

2 tablespoons lemon juice

Grated zest of one lemon

2 eggs

⅓ cup (75 ml) milk

⅔ cup (170 g) sugar

1 cup (125 g) all-purpose flour

1 teaspoon baking powder

1 teaspoon salt

½ cup (65 g) pecans

LEMON GLAZE

½ cup (75 g) powdered sugar

2 teaspoons lemon juice

Preheat oven to 350°F (180°C). In a heavy saucepan, melt the butter and simmer with the chopped ginger for 1 minute; set aside to cool. In a separate bowl, whisk the lemon juice with the zest, eggs, and milk. Sift the dry ingredients together, then stir into the batter. Stir in the ginger butter, then fold in the pecans. Pour the batter into a lightly oiled 8-inch loaf pan. Center the pan on a baking sheet and bake for 30 to 40 minutes or until a skewer comes out clean. Place the bread on a rack to cool. Make the glaze by whisking together the powdered sugar and lemon juice. Pierce the bread in several places and ladle on the glaze until fully absorbed.

Makes one 8-inch loaf

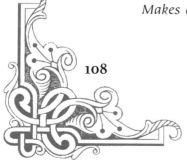

BOURSIN CHEESE MUFFINS

The boursin cheese must be prepared the day before you plan to make the muffins.

BOURSIN CHEESE

8 ounces (230 g) cream cheese

4 tablespoons (55 g) unsalted butter

1 teaspoon water

1 teaspoon white vinegar

1 teaspoon Worcestershire sauce

3 crushed garlic cloves

½ teaspoon each dried thyme, oregano, rosemary,
   marjoram, basil, dill, sage, and parsley

MUFFINS

2 cups (270 g) whole wheat pastry flour

2 cups (220 g) oat bran

2 teaspoons baking powder

1 teaspoon baking soda

1 teaspoon salt

2 eggs

1 cup (170 g) boursin cheese

2 cups (500 ml) buttermilk

¼ cup (50 ml) canola oil

To make the boursin cheese, whip the cream cheese and butter until fluffy, about 10 minutes. Add the remaining ingredients and mix until thoroughly incorporated. Refrigerate overnight.

For muffins, preheat oven to 350°F (180°C). Whisk together the dry ingredients. In a separate bowl, whisk together the eggs, cheese, buttermilk, and oil. Fold the dry ingredients into the egg batter. Scoop into a lightly oiled muffin tin and bake for about 25 minutes, or until golden brown. Serve with the remaining cheese.

109

Makes 12 muffins

SEVENTH HEAVEN BRAN MUFFINS

Feeling like a little cherub lately? These muffins (which remain moist and fresh for days) are healthful, delicious, and a filling treat for those who want to lose weight.

2 cups (270 g) whole wheat pastry flour

2 cups (220 g) oat bran

⅓ cup (60 g) packed light brown sugar

1 teaspoon cinnamon

2 teaspoons baking soda

1 teaspoon baking powder

2 cups (500 ml) buttermilk

6 tablespoons (75 ml) molasses

2 eggs

¼ cup (50 ml) canola oil

2 cups (175 g) finely grated carrot

⅔ cup (110 g) raisins or chopped dried dates

½ cup (65 g) sliced almonds

Preheat oven to 400°F (200°C) and lightly oil a muffin tin. Mix all of the dry ingredients in a bowl. In a separate bowl, whisk the buttermilk with the molasses, eggs, and oil. Stir in the carrots and raisins or dates. Fold the dry ingredients into the batter until fully moistened. Using a 4-ounce (120-g) ice cream scoop, portion the batter into the muffin cups in equal portions. Sprinkle with sliced almonds. Bake for about 20 minutes or until the muffins are golden brown and the tops spring back when lightly touched. Cool for 5 minutes before removing from muffin tin.

Makes 12 muffins

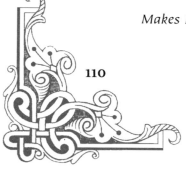

BLISSFUL BLUEBERRY MUFFINS

CRUMBLE TOPPING

3 tablespoons (25 g) all-purpose flour

3 tablespoons (50 g) sugar

¼ teaspoon cinnamon

¼ cup (30 g) slivered almonds

3 tablespoons (45 g) unsalted butter

MUFFINS

2 cups (500 ml) fresh blueberries

Touch of all-purpose flour for dusting the berries

2 eggs

½ cup (125 ml) buttermilk

¼ cup (50 ml) canola oil

½ teaspoon almond extract

¼ cup (65 g) sugar

1 teaspoon finely grated lemon zest

2 cups (250 g) all-purpose flour

1 teaspoon baking powder

½ teaspoon baking soda

¼ teaspoon salt

Preheat oven to 375°F (190°C) and lightly oil 12 muffin cups. Make the crumble topping by processing the flour, sugar, cinnamon, and almonds until the almonds are broken into small pieces. Slice the butter into 8 pieces, then process with the flour to a coarse grain. Set aside.

In a small bowl, dust 1½ cups (375 ml) of the blueberries with some flour and set aside. Whisk the eggs with the buttermilk, oil, almond extract, sugar, and lemon zest. Mash the remaining ½ cup of blueberries into the batter until creamy. Sift the flour with the baking powder, soda, and salt, then mix into the batter. Gently stir in the blueberries. Fill muffin cups three quarters full and sprinkle topping over the batter. Bake for about 20 minutes or until golden brown.

Makes 12 muffins

CHOCOLATE CHIP MUFFINS WITH CHOCOLATE BUTTER

MUFFINS

½ cup (125 ml) canola oil

1 cup (250 g) sugar

2 eggs

1 cup (250 ml) buttermilk

1 teaspoon almond extract

2 cups (250 g) all-purpose flour

½ cup (55 g) unsweetened cocoa powder

½ teaspoon baking soda

½ teaspoon baking powder

½ teaspoon salt

½ cup (100 g) chocolate chips

⅓ cup (40 g) sliced almonds

CHOCOLATE BUTTER

½ cup (125 g) unsalted butter

½ cup (75 g) sifted powdered sugar

2 tablespoons (20 g) sifted unsweetened cocoa powder

2 tablespoons heavy cream

Preheat oven to 350°F (180°C). Whisk the oil with the white and brown sugars, eggs, buttermilk, and almond extract until smooth. Sift the dry ingredients together, then stir into the egg batter. Fold in the chocolate chips. Lightly oil a muffin tin and divide the batter into 12 equal portions. Sprinkle the sliced almonds over the top. Bake for 20 minutes or until tops of muffins bounce back when lightly touched.

While the muffins are baking, whip the butter until fluffy and almost white in color. Gradually whip in the powdered sugar and the cocoa powder. Add the cream and whip until slightly glossy. (Chocolate butter can be frozen in an airtight container for several weeks. Just whip it again before serving.) Serve each muffin with a scoop of chocolate butter.

Makes 12 muffins

The Eighth Choir: Archangels
Overlighting Angels

*A*rchangels inspire us by reflecting the light of our divinity. They are actively present in all nine choirs of angels, and are working closely with us as we move toward the golden age of enlightenment. When you pray for guidance, ask for Michael, Rafael, Uriel, or Gabriel, who will come immediately to your side.

ꙮ *Michael, whose name means "He who is like God," is the prince of light. Michael holds the keys to the kingdom of heaven and guides us on our path of love to eternal light. He is the keeper and protector of virtues, and he appears in the light of sapphire blue, holding a sword.*

Rafael, whose name means "God Heals," bears the transformative fire that brings perfection to our hearts, minds, and bodies so we will awaken to our perfect divinity. We can see him in our inner vision, where he appears in the light of emerald green.

Uriel, whose name means "Fire of God," gives us prophetic understanding and insights into all worldly and personal issues, while guiding us to the great awakening. He brings insights on all worldly issues. He is the minister of grace and appears in the color of ruby.

Gabriel, whose name means "Strength of God," gives us hope when we need it most. He is the guardian of our feelings and expressions of creativity. He reveals that we are one with God and all that exists in creation. He is the angel of ascension and appears in the light of brilliant white.

↩ Table of Contents

Chapter 8
Sinless Sorbets and Enlightened Ice Creams

About Sorbets

When making a sorbet, it is best to use seasonal ripe fruits; however, frozen fruit may be substituted. The traditional method of sorbet making is to purée the fruit of choice, then purée it again with simple syrup for sweetness and consistency.

I have also found that in place of simple syrup, fruit juice concentrate gives the sorbet additional flavor and a delightfully creamy texture. White grape juice maintains a fairly neutral taste and gives a lot of sweetness. Some of the more exotic flavors are fun to play with: try guava or passion fruit, as well as concentrates that combine several different types of juice. Freezing diminishes the sweetness of the sorbet, so keep this in mind when tasting the mixture before final processing.

STILL FREEZE METHOD

Process the fruit to a purée. If you are making a berry sorbet, run the purée through a sieve to remove the seeds. Process again with sweetener and flavor enhancers. Freeze in a covered shallow dish until it is firm around the edges and slushy in the center. Process again until smooth. Add the liqueur, if desired. Return the mixture to the freezer until the sorbet is firm, yet smooth and creamy. If the sorbet becomes too hard, let it rest in the refrigerator.

SORBETIERE OR ICE CREAM-MAKER METHOD

Process the fruit to a purée. If you are making a berry sorbet, run the purée through a sieve to remove the seeds. Process again with the sweetener and flavor enhancers. Chill until cold. Freeze according to manufacturer's instructions. If using a liqueur, add it during the last minute of the freezing process, because the alcohol will slow the process. Return the sorbet to the freezer in a covered dish until firm.

Each sorbet recipe listed in this chapter works with either of the above methods.

$\mathcal{S}$IMPLE SYRUP

Simple syrup is the secret to making sorbet with the proper sweetness and consistency.

Equal parts water and sugar

In a heavy saucepan, stir the sugar and water over medium heat until the sugar is dissolved, then simmer for 10 minutes. Cool before using. Simple syrup can be stored covered in the refrigerator for up to one month.

For vanilla syrup, add a split vanilla bean to the sugar water before boiling and keep the pod in the sugar water when storing it.

$\mathcal{R}$ASPBERRY PEACH SORBET

12 ounces (340 g) raspberries, fresh or frozen

2 cups (500 ml) peach puree

1 cup (250 ml) amaretto-flavored syrup

¼ cup (50 ml) lemon juice

Puree the raspberries and run them through a sieve to remove the seeds. Purée again with the peach purée, syrup, and lemon juice until smooth. Refrigerate until cold, then process as directed on page 117.

Makes 4 cups (1 litre)

SUNBURST STRAWBERRY SORBET

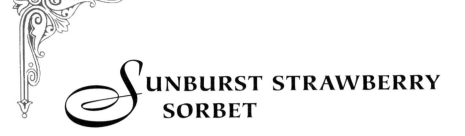

4 cups (1 litre) strawberries

1 cup (250 ml) orange juice

1½ cups (225 g) powdered sugar

2 tablespoons lemon juice

Clean and hull the strawberries. Purée the fruit with the orange juice, powdered sugar, and lemon juice. Refrigerate until cold, then process as directed on page 117.

Makes 4 cups (1 litre)

REVELATION OF RASPBERRY SORBET

3 cups (750 ml) raspberries

1 cup (250 ml) simple syrup

1 cup (250 ml) orange juice

½ teaspoon almond extract

2 tablespoons Chambord (optional)

Purée the raspberries and run them through a sieve to remove the seeds. Purée again with the simple syrup, orange juice, and almond extract. Refrigerate until cold, then process as directed on page 117, adding the Chambord during the final stages of freezing, if desired.

Makes 4 cups (1 litre)

LEMON AND ORANGE FLOWER WATER SORBET

1 cup (250 ml) lemon juice

2 teaspoons finely grated lemon zest

1 tablespoon orange flower water

2 cups (500 ml) simple syrup

Whisk together the lemon juice, zest, orange flower water, and simple syrup. Refrigerate until cold, then process as directed on page 117.

Makes 3 cups (750 ml)

LIME AND ROSE WATER SORBET

1 cup (250 ml) lime juice

½ cup (125 ml) lemon juice

1 tablespoon rose water

3 cups (750 ml) simple syrup

Whisk together the lemon juice, lime juice, rose water, and simple syrup. Refrigerate until cold, then process as directed on page 117.

Makes 4½ cups (1 litre)

LACKBERRY PEACH SORBET

4 cups (1 litre) blackberries

2 cups (500 ml) peach slices

1 cup (250 ml) white grape juice concentrate

Purée the blackberries and run them through a sieve to remove the seeds. Purée again with the peaches and white grape juice. Refrigerate until cold, then process as directed on page 117.

Makes 4½ cups (1 litre)

ERY CHERRY SORBET

1 pound (454 g) dark sweet pitted cherries,
   fresh or frozen

12 ounces (340 g) frozen cherry juice concentrate

⅓ cup (50 g) powdered sugar

1 cup (250 ml) water

1 teaspoon almond extract

¼ cup (50 ml) mandarin orange liqueur or
   mandarin orange-flavored syrup

Purée the cherries to a smooth paste. Purée again with the remaining ingredients, except the liqueur or syrup, until well blended. Refrigerate until cold, then process as directed on page 117. In the final stages of freezing, add the liqueur or syrup.

Makes 5 cups (1¼ litres)

$\mathcal{L}$YCHEE COCONUT SORBET

Lychees can be found at most Chinese grocery stores and some supermarkets. Cóco Lopez is cream of coconut, which is used to make piña coladas.

20-ounce (565-g) can lychees in heavy syrup

15-ounce (425-g) can Cóco Lopez

1 tablespoon vanilla extract

Purée the lychees and syrup until creamy. Purée again with the Cóco Lopez and vanilla until smooth. Refrigerate until cold, then process as directed above.

Makes 4 cups (1 litre)

$\mathcal{C}$HOCOLATE SORBET

4 cups (1 litre) water

1½ cups (375 g) sugar

4 ounces (120 g) unsweetened chocolate, chopped

¼ cup fresh chopped mint (optional)

In a heavy saucepan, boil the water and sugar for 10 minutes. Add the chocolate and gently simmer an additional 5 minutes. Cool to room temperature and combine with fresh mint, if desired. Refrigerate until cold, then process as directed above.

Makes 5 cups (1¼ litres)

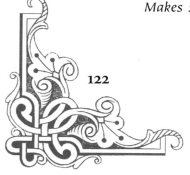

HAI COFFEE ICE

3 cups (750 ml) strong coffee

1 cup (250 ml) light cream

1 cup (250 g) sugar

1 teaspoon vanilla extract

In a heavy saucepan, combine the coffee, cream, and sugar. Over low heat, stir until the sugar is dissolved. Add the vanilla and cool to room temperature. Refrigerate until cold, then process as directed above.

Makes 4½ cups (1 litre)

HAI TEA ICE

2 cups (500 ml) water

1 cinnamon stick

1 teaspoon allspice seeds

1 teaspoon cardamom seeds

1 teaspoon fenugreek seeds

¼ teaspoon whole black pepper

1 cup (250 g) sugar

5 black tea bags

1 cup (250 ml) heavy cream

In a heavy saucepan, whisk the first seven ingredients together and bring to a boil. Simmer for an additional 10 minutes, then remove from heat. Add the tea bags and allow to steep for 20 minutes, covered. Strain the liquid, then stir in the cream. Refrigerate until cold, then process as directed above.

Makes 3 cups (750 ml)

About Ice Cream

Egg yolks used in ice cream must be cooked to eliminate possible bacterial growth. The temperature of the custard should reach 180°F (82°C) on a candy thermometer, which requires about 10 minutes of stirring over low heat to achieve.

Always cool the ice cream custard in the refrigerator before freezing so that optimal hardening will be achieved with your choice of machine. Ice cream will reach a peak of flavor if transferred to the freezer for at least 1 hour before serving. For a truly angelic dessert, try anointing your homemade ice cream with a sacred sauce.

MANGO ICE CREAM

1 cup (250 g) sugar, divided

2 egg yolks

2 cups (500 ml) heavy cream

1 tablespoon finely grated orange zest

¾ cup (232 g) mango purée

1 teaspoon almond extract

½ cup (125 ml) mango-flavored syrup (optional)

In a small bowl, whisk half the sugar with the egg yolks. In a heavy saucepan, mix the cream with the remaining sugar and orange zest and heat just to the boiling point. Remove from heat and, in a steady stream, pour the hot cream over the egg yolks while whisking vigorously. Return the mixture to the saucepan over low heat. Cook the custard while whisking constantly for 10 minutes; do not allow the mixture to boil. Remove from heat and whisk in the mango purée, almond extract, and mango syrup. Cool to room temperature, then refrigerate overnight. Freeze according to the manufacturer's instructions. Scoop into a bowl, cover, and freeze until firm.

124

Makes 4 cups (1 litre)

COFFEE TOFFEE CHIP ICE CREAM

*Try serving scoops of this divine ice cream on tuilles with
Mocha or Espresso Sauce (pages 59 and 58).*

1 cup (250 g) sugar

¼ cup (50 ml) water

⅔ cup (160 ml) strong coffee or espresso

¼ cup (50 ml) light corn syrup

2 cups (500 ml) heavy cream

4 egg yolks

2 tablespoons vanilla extract

½ cup (100 g) shaved semisweet chocolate

In a heavy saucepan, stir the sugar and water until dissolved. Over medium heat, boil without stirring until the sugar is amber-colored and caramelized. Remove from heat and slowly whisk in the coffee combined with the light corn syrup. If the caramel seizes, return to heat and stir until dissolved. In a separate bowl, whisk together the cream and egg yolks. While whisking vigorously, pour the hot coffee mixture into the cream in a thin steady stream. Return to low heat and cook the custard, stirring, for about 10 minutes or until it coats the back of a spoon. Add the vanilla, cool to room temperature, and chill until cold. Freeze according to the manufacturer's instructions. At the last minute of freezing, incorporate the chocolate shavings. Scoop into a bowl, cover, and freeze until firm.

Makes 4 cups (1 litre)

CHOCOLATE RASPBERRY DIVINE

*For a rich, deep chocolate ice cream that stands well
by itself, just omit the raspberries.*

10 ounces (285 g) semisweet chocolate

1 cup (250 ml) heavy cream

4 egg yolks

1 cup (250 g) sugar

1½ cups (375 ml) milk

10 ounces (285 g) frozen raspberries in heavy syrup, thawed

Melt the chocolate with the cream and set aside. In a separate bowl, whisk the egg yolks with the sugar until light and lemon-colored. In a heavy saucepan, bring the milk just to the boiling point, then, whisking vigorously, pour it over the egg yolks in a thin stream. Return to low heat and cook the custard while continuing to stir for about 10 minutes. Remove from heat and whisk in the chocolate, then add the raspberries and syrup. Cool, then freeze according to the manufacturer's instructions. Scoop into a bowl, cover, and freeze until firm.

Makes 5 cups (1¼ litres)

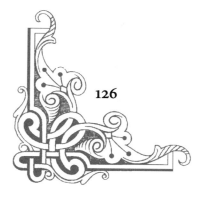

HEAVENLY WHITE CHOCOLATE ICE CREAM

This is quite simply the best ice cream I have ever tasted!

1 vanilla bean, split

1 cup (250 ml) milk

10 ounces (285 g) white chocolate

⅓ cup (75 ml) sour cream, at room temperature

4 egg yolks

¾ cup (190 g) sugar

2 cups (500 ml) heavy cream

½ cup (65 g) crushed pistachio nuts (optional)

Split the vanilla bean lengthwise and allow it to marinate with the milk in a heavy saucepan for 15 minutes. Meanwhile, melt the white chocolate, then whisk in the sour cream and set aside. In a separate bowl, whisk the egg yolks with the sugar until light and lemon-colored.

Bring the milk just to the boiling point and discard the vanilla bean. In a steady stream, pour the milk into the egg yolks while whisking vigorously. Return to heat and cook the custard for about 10 minutes while continuing to whisk. Remove from heat and stir in the white chocolate mixture and the heavy cream. Cool, then freeze according to manufacturer's instructions. Add the crushed pistachios toward the end of the freezing process, if desired.

Makes 4½ cups (1 litre)

About Gelato

Of all the Italian desserts, gelato is my favorite. Gelato is "still frozen," not whipped, so the ice cream has a denser texture with fewer air bubbles. The sweetened condensed milk binds the flavors and adds richness to these recipes. These recipes require no cooking, and no eggs are added.

AMARETTO GELATO

½ cup (80 g) chopped dried apricots

½ cup (125 ml) Amaretto or amaretto-flavored syrup

17-ounce (480-g) can sweetened condensed milk

2 cups (500 ml) heavy cream

Soak the chopped apricots with the Amaretto or syrup for a half hour. Whisk in the condensed milk, then the heavy cream. Pour into a container, cover, and freeze until firm.

Makes 4½ cups (1 litre)

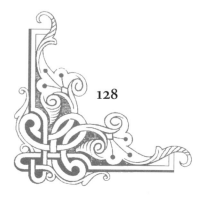

CHOCOLATE LIQUEUR GELATO

6 ounces (170 g) bittersweet chocolate

¾ cup (175 ml) liqueur (Frangelico, Amaretto, Irish Cream, Grand Marnier) or flavored syrup

½ cup (200 g) sweetened condensed milk

2 cups (500 ml) heavy cream

Melt the chocolate with the liqueur or syrup; set aside to cool. Whisk in the sweetened condensed milk, then the heavy cream. Pour into a container, cover, and freeze until firm.

Makes 3 cups (750 ml)

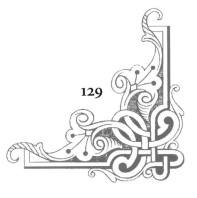

The Ninth Choir:
Guardian Angels
Divine Companions

A guardian angel has walked by your side from the moment you were born. Our personal angels can be our best friends and spiritual mentors if we are open to their celestial guidance. They are a brilliant light shining divine love on us with thoughts of faith, trust, healing, and, of course, inspiration. Our guardian angels touch us through intuition, thought, and heavenly force, when needed. They spend less time guarding us and greater moments lifting us on their wings of higher consciousness to the realization of our own angelic nature. They appear in all colors and are supremely beautiful.

During the summer I used to go to a beautiful lake in the national forest to pray and meditate. In a moment when my mind was very still, three incredibly tall angels appeared before me. My heart opened like a faucet and a sense of pure love poured through me. I heard an angelic voice that filled everything saying, "Love with all your might." Radiant love filled everything around me while these beautiful angels gave me guidance and encouragement. When they disappeared I felt serenity and love more powerful than I knew was possible. My heart remained open for several months, which nurtured and comforted me beyond words. —Orphiel

✆ Table of Contents

Chapter 9
More Divine Desserts

CHOCOLATE PATÉ

4 tablespoons (55 g) unsalted butter

1 cup (250 ml) heavy cream

15 ounces (425 g) bittersweet chocolate

4 egg yolks

1 cup (150 g) sifted powdered sugar

¼ cup (50 ml) Frangelico or hazelnut-flavored syrup

Cocoa powder for dusting

In a heavy saucepan over low heat, melt the butter with the cream, then stir in the chocolate until melted. Remove from heat and whisk in the egg yolks one at a time. Whisk in the powdered sugar, then the liqueur or syrup.

Line an 8 x 4-inch loaf pan with clear food wrap and pour in the chocolate ganache to fill. Pull the wrap to cover the chocolate and gently fold over. Refrigerate overnight. To remove from the pan, gently pull on the wrap from both sides; it should come out very easily. Discard the wrap and center the paté on a serving dish. Dust lightly with cocoa powder. Slice the pate into 8 portions with a knife that has been warmed in hot water and then dried with a towel. Serve on a pool of Frangelico Sauce (page 61), with a slice of Chocolate Pound Cake (page 14), if desired.

Serves 8

COSMIC ESPRESSO BROWNIES

For a truly decadent experience, serve these brownies warm with Espresso Sauce (page 58), a scoop of Coffee Toffee Chip Ice Cream (page 125), and a few chocolate-covered espresso beans.

1⅓ cups (300 g) unsalted butter

2 cups (500 g) sugar

⅓ cup (75 ml) light corn syrup

4 eggs

1 teaspoon vanilla extract

¼ cup (50 ml) Kahlua or coffee-flavored syrup

3 tablespoons (30 g) finely ground espresso beans

1½ cups (190 g) all-purpose flour

1 cup (110 g) cocoa powder

1 teaspoon salt

1 teaspoon baking powder

1 cup (200 g) chocolate chips

1 cup (125 g) pecan halves

Preheat oven to 350°F (180°C). Beat the butter with the sugar and corn syrup until light and fluffy. Beat in the eggs one at a time, mixing well. Add the vanilla and the Kahlua or coffee-flavored syrup. Whisk the espresso beans, flour, cocoa powder, salt, and baking powder together, then beat into the batter. Pour into a lightly oiled 13 x 9-inch rectangular pan, sprinkle on the pecans and chocolate chips, and bake for about 40 to 45 minutes. Do not over-cook. Brownies are best when slightly underbaked; they firm up while cooling.

Serves 12 to 16

LOVELY BERRY CRUMBLE

APPLE BERRY FILLING

3 Red Delicious apples, peeled, cored, and sliced thin

1 pint (300 g) strawberries, hulled and sliced

1 pound (454 g) blackberries, fresh or frozen

1 pound (454 g) blueberries, fresh or frozen

1 cup (250 g) sugar

½ cup (165 g) seedless blackberry jam

1 teaspoon almond extract

1 tablespoon orange flower water

½ cup (65 g) all-purpose flour

CRUMBLE TOPPING

¾ cup (175 g) unsalted butter

1¼ cups (215 g) packed light brown sugar

1 cup (125 g) all-purpose flour

½ cup (65 g) pecans

Preheat oven to 375°F (190°C). In a large bowl, combine the fruit. Sprinkle the sugar over the top and toss with a large spoon or with your hands. In a small bowl, whisk the blackberry jam with the almond extract and orange flower water. Mix with the fruit, and toss one more time. Sprinkle the flour over the fruit and toss until the flour is evenly dispersed.

To make the topping, cut the butter with the brown sugar. Process with the remaining ingredients until crumbly. To assemble, place a 13 x 9-inch rectangular dish on a baking sheet. Turn the berry mixture into the dish. Smother with the crumble topping and bake for 60 to 70 minutes at 375°F (190°C) or until the top is browned and juices are bubbling over.

Serves 8 to 12

BLUEBERRY CHERRY CRUMBLE

CRUMBLE TOPPING

¾ cup (165 g) unsalted butter

1 cup (170 g) packed light brown sugar

1 cup (125 g) all-purpose flour

1 cup (125 g) sliced almonds

BLUEBERRY CHERRY FILLING

5 cups or 1½ pounds (660 g) blueberries

1 pound (454 g) pitted dark sweet cherries

1 teaspoon almond extract

Juice and finely grated zest of 1 orange

½ cup (125 g) sugar

½ cup (65 g) all-purpose flour

Preheat oven to 375°F (190°C). Prepare the topping by processing the butter, brown sugar, and flour until crumbly. Process with the almonds to break them into small pieces. Set aside. In a large bowl, combine the fruits and toss with the almond extract mixed with the orange juice and zest. Toss the fruits with the sugar, then add the flour. Turn out onto an 11 x 7½-inch rectangular baking dish. Firmly press the crumble topping to cover. Place the dish on a baking sheet and bake for about 1 hour or until the juices are seeping through the topping. Serve warm with a scoop of vanilla ice cream, if desired.

Serves 6

LAVENDER CRÈME BRÛLÉE

3 cups (750 ml) heavy cream

1 tablespoon (10 g) dried lavender blossoms

Zest of 1 orange

8 egg yolks

½ cup (125 g) sugar

4 ounces (120 g) white chocolate, broken into small pieces

GLAZE

6 tablespoons (65 g) packed light brown sugar

Preheat oven to 300°F (150°C). In a heavy saucepan, heat the cream, lavender, and orange zest just to the boiling point. Remove from heat and steep, covered, for 15 minutes. Whisk the egg yolks with the sugar until light and lemon-colored. Return the cream to a simmer, then pour it over the egg yolks in a thin stream while whisking vigorously. Whisk in the white chocolate until melted, then pour the mixture through a fine sieve.

Place six ½-cup ramekins in a large roasting pan and fill it with hot water to halfway up the sides of the ramekins. Divide the cream mixture evenly among the ramekins. Tent a piece of aluminum foil over the roasting pan, then carefully set in the center of the preheated oven. Bake for 45 minutes and check to see if the center is set. It should tremble when touched, but should not be liquid and loose. If necessary, remove the foil and bake until set. Remove the brûlée from the water bath and allow to cool before chilling in the refrigerator. When fully chilled, sprinkle the tops of the custards with the brown sugar and place under a broiler for 2 minutes, or until the sugar caramelizes. Serve on a plate sprinkled with more dried lavender blossoms.

Serves 6

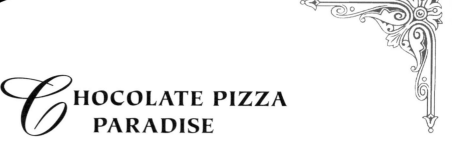

$\mathcal{C}$HOCOLATE PIZZA PARADISE

This "pizza" needs to freeze overnight, so be sure to begin preparations the day before you plan to serve it.

CRUST

3 cups (330 g) chocolate cookies with
   cream filling, ground fine

½ cup (125 g) unsalted butter

FUDGE BATTER

1 cup (225 g) unsalted butter

12 ounces (340 g) semisweet chocolate

1 cup (250 g) sugar

¼ cup (50 ml) grenadine

4 eggs

3 tablespoons (25 g) all-purpose flour

TOPPING

½ cup (165 g) seedless raspberry jam

¼ cup (50 ml) light corn syrup

2 tablespoons Triple Sec or orange juice

4 cups (1 l) assorted sliced fruits: peaches,
   blueberries, raspberries, bananas, pears, etc.

8 strawberries, hulled

2 ounces (60 g) white chocolate, melted

1 cup (200 g) semisweet chocolate shavings

138

Lightly oil the bottom and sides of a 10-inch diameter, 3-inch deep cake pan, then dust with flour. Mix the cookie crumbs with the melted butter, then press to cover the bottom and sides of the cake pan. Refrigerate.

Preheat oven to 350°F (180°C). In a heavy saucepan melt the butter with the chocolate while stirring constantly. Remove from heat and whisk in the sugar and grenadine until smooth. Whisk in the eggs one at a time, then add the flour. Pour the batter over the chocolate crust and center the pan on a cookie sheet. Bake for 20 minutes. Set on rack to cool. (It may appear slightly separated but it will firm up beautifully.) Refrigerate until cold, then freeze overnight. To remove from the pan, run a sharp knife around the edges of the pizza, flip over onto a plate, then turn right side up; center on a serving platter.

To assemble, spread the raspberry jam over the top of the cake. Whisk the light corn syrup with the Triple Sec or juice. Toss with the sliced fruit, then spread the fruit over the top of the pizza. Press the hulled strawberries flat with the bottom of a glass (to resemble pepperoni). Scatter over the glazed fruit. Garnish with dribbles of melted white chocolate (to resemble melted cheese), then sprinkle with dark chocolate shavings. Cut into wedges and serve.

Serves 12

ALMOND OR HAZELNUT PRALINE

This crushed praline can be sprinkled over cakes, tarts, truffles, and ice creams.

½ cup (125 ml) water

1 tablespoon lemon juice

2 cups (500 g) sugar

1 cup (125 g) almonds or hazelnuts, skinned

In a heavy saucepan over medium heat, stir the water, lemon juice, and sugar until dissolved. Without stirring, boil the mixture until light amber in color, approximately 10 minutes. Remove from heat, add the nuts, and stir until the foam subsides. Turn the mixture onto an oiled marble slab or lightly oiled baking sheet. In about an hour, when the praline has cooled and hardened, break it into pieces. Process to a fine powder and store in an airtight container for up to 3 months.

Makes 2½ cups

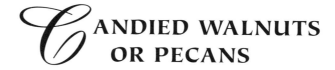

CANDIED WALNUTS OR PECANS

4 tablespoons (55 g) unsalted butter

2 cups (250 g) walnuts or pecans

⅓ cup (60 g) packed light brown sugar

In a heavy frying pan, melt the butter over medium heat. Add the nuts and stir for 5 minutes until lightly browned. Add the brown sugar and stir until the nuts are coated. Continue to cook, stirring, for 3 minutes. Turn onto a baking sheet and allow to cool while breaking up into pieces. Store in an airtight container for up to 3 weeks.

Makes 2½ cups

AMARETTO CRÈME CARAMEL

CARAMEL

½ cup (125 ml) water

1 teaspoon lemon juice

1 cup (250 g) sugar

CUSTARD

8 eggs

4 egg yolks

1 cup (250 g) sugar

1 quart (1 l) half-and-half

½ cup (125 ml) Amaretto or amaretto-flavored syrup

1 teaspoon almond extract

GARNISH

8 to 10 strawberries

Preheat oven to 350°F (180°C). In a heavy saucepan over moderate heat, stir the water, lemon, and sugar until dissolved. Without stirring, boil the mixture until golden caramel in color, then pour into a slightly warmed 10-inch cake pan. Set aside while preparing the custard. In a large bowl, whisk together the eggs, extra yolks, and sugar. Whisk in the half-and-half, then the Amaretto or flavored syrup. Add the almond extract, then strain through a sieve. Pour the custard gently over the back of a large spoon into the pan over the caramelized sugar.

Place the crème caramel in a large roasting pan, then pour in enough hot water to reach halfway up the sides of the cake pan. Center in the oven, then immediately reduce the temperature to 325°F (160°C) and bake for about 1 hour. To test for doneness, insert a knife into the center. It should come out clean. Cool on a rack, then refrigerate for at least 4 hours. To remove, run a sharp knife around the edges of the custard; place the serving platter over the top and invert. Thinly slice the strawberries up to the hull, then press into fan shapes. Place on top of the custard as a garnish.

Serves 8 to 10

IRAMISU OF MY DREAMS

FRANGELICO SABAYON

6 egg yolks

⅓ cup (85 g) sugar

½ cup (125 ml) Frangelico or hazelnut-flavored syrup

MASCARPONE CREAM

2 cups (450 g) mascarpone cheese

2 cups (500 ml) heavy cream

¾ cup (115 g) powdered sugar

1 teaspoon vanilla extract

¼ cup (30 g) crushed toasted hazelnuts

¼ cup (50 g) flaked semisweet chocolate

½ cup (125 ml) freshly brewed espresso, cooled

¼ cup (50 ml) Amaretto or amaretto-flavored syrup

1 Chocolate Pound Cake (pg 14)

GARNISH

Chocolate shavings or cocoa

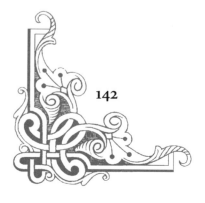

To make the sabayon, whip the egg yolks with the sugar until thick and yellow, about 5 minutes. Place over a bowl of lightly simmering water and whisk in the Frangelico or syrup until the mixture triples in volume and holds soft peaks, about 3 minutes. Remove from the heat and continue whipping until the mixture has cooled, approximately 5 minutes.

Beat the mascarpone for 1 minute to lighten, then set aside. Whip the cream with the powdered sugar and vanilla extract to soft peaks. Add the mascarpone and whip until the mixture holds stiff peaks. Whip with the hazelnuts and chocolate until evenly dispersed. Note: If you can't find mascarpone, use this substitute: Beat 11 ounces (330 g) of cream cheese with ¾ cup (175 ml) heavy cream and refrigerate for 1 day before using.

To assemble, mix the espresso and Amaretto. Slice half of the cake into ¼-inch (4 mm) strips. (The other half of the cake is not needed for this dish.) Arrange one layer to cover the bottom of a 13 x 9 x 3-inch cake pan. Brush on half of the coffee mixture. Layer half of the mascarpone on top. Spread half of the Frangelico Sabayon to cover. Repeat the process with the second layer. Sprinkle generously with grated chocolate or dust with cocoa powder. Refrigerate for at least 4 hours to allow flavors to blend.

Serves 12

CANNOLI

This is a labor-intensive dish, but it's worth it! Cafe Sport in San Francisco gave me the secret years ago—the almond extract—and I've been a junkie ever since. You will need 5½ x 1-inch cannoli forms for this recipe.

SHELLS

1 ¾ cups (220 g) all-purpose flour

2 tablespoons sugar

½ teaspoon salt

2 teaspoons finely grated lemon zest

2 tablespoons (30 g) unsalted butter

1 egg

¼ cup (50 ml) dry white wine

1 egg white

Oil for deep frying

RICOTTA FILLING

30 ounces (850 g) ricotta cheese

½ cup (125 ml) whipping cream

1 ½ cups (225 g) powdered sugar

1 teaspoon almond extract

1 cup (200 g) mini chocolate chips, or 1 cup (160 g) candied fruits

GARNISHES FOR DIPPING

1 cup (200 g) chocolate shavings

1 cup (125 g) coarsely chopped pistachios

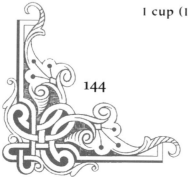

To make the shells, combine flour, sugar, salt, and lemon zest, then process with butter to a coarse grain. Process with the whole egg and wine to form a fairly stiff dough. Cover with clear food wrap and allow to stand covered at room temperature for 30 minutes.

On a floured board, roll out 3½-inch rounds, to ¹/₁₆-inch thickness, then wrap the dough around the cannoli forms and seal with the egg white. Deep fry in hot oil for 1 minute or until golden brown. Drain on a paper towel and cool before removing the shell from the metal tube to dry on a paper towel. Repeat until all of the dough is cooked.

To make the filling, whisk the ricotta cheese with the cream, powdered sugar, and almond extract until smooth. Stir in the mini chocolate chips or candied fruits. When the shells are cooled, pipe or spoon the filling into the shells. Dip one side into the chocolate shavings and the other into the chopped pistachios. Refrigerate until ready to serve. Dust lightly with powdered sugar just before serving.

Makes about 24 cannoli

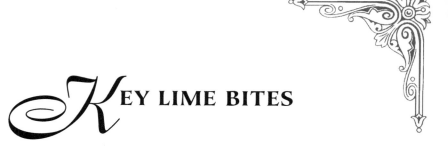

$\mathcal{K}$EY LIME BITES

CRUST

3½ cups (380 g) lemon or graham cracker crumbs

½ cup (125 g) melted unsalted butter

KEY LIME FILLING

Two 14-ounce (792-g) cans sweetened condensed milk

6 egg yolks

1 cup (250 ml) key lime juice

GLAZE

Orange Sour Cream Sauce (page 62)

Mix the crumbs with the melted butter and press into a 13 x 9-inch rectangular baking dish. Bake at 350°F (180°C) for 10 minutes or until the edges are lightly browned. In the meantime, whisk the sweetened condensed milk with the yolks and key lime juice. Pour the batter over the prebaked crust and return to the oven for an additional 5 minutes. While mixture is baking, prepare the sauce. Smooth the sauce over the top and bake for 2 more minutes. Cool on a rack, then refrigerate until cold, at least 4 hours. Cut into bars and serve on a plate with sliced lime rounds.

Makes about 32 bars

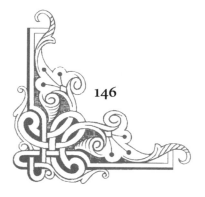

METRIC CONVERSIONS

LOVING SPOONFULS

1 tablespoon = 15 ml   2 tablespoons = 25 ml

1 teaspoon = 5 ml

½ teaspoon = 2.5 ml

¼ teaspoon = 1.25 ml

CAKE PANS

Angel Food Cake Pan: 9½ x 4 inch = 24 x 10 cm

Round: 10 x 2 inch = 25 x 5 cm

Round: 9 x 2 inch = 23 x 5 cm

Springform: 9 x 3 inch = 23 x 8 cm

Square: 8 x 8 x 2 inch = 20 x 20 x 5 cm

Small Rectangular: 11 x 7½ x 2 inch = 28 x 19 x 5 cm

Large Rectangular: 13 x 9 x 2 inch = 33 x 23 x 5 cm

BREAD PANS

Loaf: 8 x 4 x 2½ inch = 20 x 10 x 6½ cm

Loaf: 9 x 5½ x 3 inch = 23 x 24 x 8 cm

Tube: 12 x 5 x 3 inch = 30 x 13 x 8 cm

TART PANS

4 x 1 inch round = 10 x 2½ cm

10 x 1 inch round = 25 x 2½ cm

PIE PANS

9 x 2 inch round = 23 x 5 cm

10 x 2¼ inch round deep dish = 25 x 6 cm

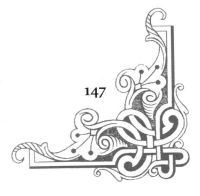